The Visitation

A monastic way of life in the Church

Éditions du Signe

Éditions du Signe
1, rue Alfred Kastler- Eckbolsheim
B.P. 94 – 67038 Strasbourg, Cedex 2, France
Tel : ++33 (03) 88 78 91 91
Fax : ++33 (03) 88 78 91 99
www.editionsdusigne.fr
email : info@editionsdusigne.fr

Layout : Éditions du Signe - 107846
Pictures : Images contributed by Visitation monasteries
and A. Robert McGilvray, OSFS;
US photography by John Glover
Front cover: © Elleb - Fotolia.com
Back cover: © Fiddich - Fotolia.com

© Éditions du Signe, 2008
ISBN 978-2-7468-2091-3
Printed in Singapore

• *Vincent de Paul, Francis de Sales, Louise de Marillac, Jane de Chantal, other Visitandines*

TABLE OF CONTENTS

1

INTRODUCTION
TO THE FOUNDERS

SAINT FRANCIS DE SALES

AND

SAINT JANE DE CHANTAL

SAINT FRANCIS DE SALES

• St. Francis de Sales

Significant Dates

- **Birth:** August 21, 1567 at the Castle de Sales, Thorens (near Annecy), Savoy
- **Study at University of Paris:** 1582-1588
- **Study at University of Padua:** 1589-1592
- **Ordination to Priesthood:** December 18, 1593
- **Missionary Work in the Chablais:** 1594-1597
- **Consecration as Bishop:** December 8, 1602
- *Introduction to the Devout Life:* 1608
- *Treatise on the Love of God:* 1616
- **Foundation of the Visitation:** June 6, 1610
- **Death:** December 28, 1622, at Lyons, aged 55
- **Canonization:** 1655
- **Proclamation as Doctor of the Church:** 1877

• *Monsieur and Madame de Boisy, Francis de Sales's parents*

• *Castle of the de Sales family near Thorens*

1 ▪ Francis, Youth, Student, Seeker

Francis, a French-speaking Savoyard, was the eldest in a large family of lesser nobility. His intelligence and industriousness led his father to prepare the boy for a career in law through rigorous education, culminating in doctorates of civil and canon law. The support of his mother and his prestigious appointment as Provost of the Cathedral Chapter persuaded his father to give reluctant consent to Francis's desire for service in the Church. He was ordained a priest.

As a student in Paris, studying Scripture and learning about predestination, Francis had been unable to sleep and eat, beset with the idea that he might be relegated to eternity in hell, blaspheming God.

Kneeling before an image of the Black Virgin, he prayed that if he could not love God in the afterlife, he might at least do so in the present. Francis became completely calm.

• *Black Virgin*

His optimistic and balanced conviction of God's desire for the salvation of all, born out of tremendous struggle, never left him.

2 ▪ Francis, Man of the Church

- Priest -

The young priest set out to:

Offer clear and solid teaching. He preached with strength and simplicity and slipped articles on Catholic doctrine under the residents' doors at Thonon for which he was later named patron of journalists.

Implement the decrees of the Council of Trent (completed in 1563, shortly before his birth). He recognized several needs: reform in a Church suffering grave disorders; solid faith in a society evolving new ideas (of Erasmus, Rabelais, Montaigne); modernization in a world making new discoveries (of Copernicus, Galileo).

Re-conquer Calvinist Geneva with weapons of fasting, charity, and good behavior. He urged his canons to live "as children of God, not only in name, but in reality."

- Bishop -

In his episcopal position, Francis strove to:

Educate and inspire his clergy. He promoted study of theology and service of the people through teaching and compassion. With his friend, Antoine Favre, Francis established the Florimontane Academy (precursor of the French Academy) to integrate knowledge, culture, and spirituality.

Support and enrich religious life. He devoted much effort to reform lax abbeys and monasteries. He founded the Visitation to provide broader opportunities for religious life.

Promote strong faith and knowledge. He preached zealously, always focusing on Scripture, on understanding of the Christian mysteries, on vibrant receptions of the sacraments, and on tender love of neighbor. He gave spiritual direction to many in person and through letters.

• *Portrait painted in 1618. Thorens Visitation Convent*

Reach out to all persons in his diocese. He gave special attention to women, to the poor, and to the disadvantaged. Because of his assistance to a deaf mute, Francis was later named patron of the deaf.

3 ▪ Francis, Writer

• *Manuscript and first edition*
The Introduction to the Devout Life

Francis has made his mark in French literature as one who rendered his work accessible through use of the vernacular rather than Latin. He wrote, as he apparently thought, with an abundance of figures, circling an idea over and over with different similes, much as the creature of his favorite image, the bee, might orbit a flower.

Francis would be astonished at being well known as an author since he wrote from a sense of duty under the impetus of apostolic urgency. The *Introduction* grew out of letters written as spiritual direction. The *Controversies (Meditations on* the Church) and *Defense of the Standard of the Cross* were dictated by the need to reply to Protestant misunderstanding. Even the *Treatise on the Love of God* came about in response to the Visitation Sisters, who sought guidance in deepening their spirituality.

The *Introduction* (1608) became an instant success since it gave guidelines to a growing class of educated persons for whom printed books had recently become available. The book addresses Christians who desire to live a fervent spiritual life in the midst of the world. This work is still translated, variously adapted, and published today.

The *Treatise* (1616) moves a step beyond the Introduction, addressing persons who wish to progress toward ever more loving union with God in the concrete situations in which they find themselves.

Further, the *Treatise* also illustrates, in the person of its author, the close union between action and writing.

4 ▪ Francis, Saint

Francis de Sales was revered by his daughters (the Visitation Sisters), honored by kings, and loved by children. His goodness was the quality most striking to his contemporaries.

His friend, Saint Vincent de Paul, described Francis as "the man who best reproduced the Son of God living on earth."

5 ▪ Francis, Man of Vision

The document *Saubadiae Gemma* of Pope Paul VI (1967) states:

No one of the recent Doctors of the Church more than St. Francis de Sales anticipated the deliberations and decisions of the Second Vatican Council with such a keen and progressive insight. He … has opened and strengthened the spiritual ways of Christian perfection for all states and conditions of life.

The *Introduction* insists on the call of all Christians, not merely priests and religious, to a life of holiness. The devout life finds nourishment in the word of God, sacraments, and prayer. Francis counseled women with respect and co-founded the only religious order at that time not conceived as an adjunct to an establishment for men. Within the context of his times, he taught and practiced principles of social justice and a gracious, grace-filled way of life. His spirituality, founded in Church tradition, resonates in today's world.

• Lake of Annecy

SAINT JANE DE CHANTAL

• Portrait of Jane at 20 years old.

Significant Dates

- **Birth:** January 23, 1572, in Dijon, Burgundy, France
- **Death of her Mother:** 1573
- **Residence with her Sister in Poitiers:** 1587-1592
- **Marriage to Christopher de Rabutin, Baron de Chantal:** December 29, 1592
- **Death of Christopher:** 1601
- **Residence with her Father-in-law at Monthélon:** 1603-1610
- **Meeting with Francis de Sales:** March 5, 1604
- **Choice of Francis as Director:** August 25, 1604
- **Foundation of the Visitation:** June 6, 1610
- **Death:** December 13, 1641, at Moulins, aged 69
- **Canonization:** 1767

• Burgundy, native region of Jane Frances de Chantal

• Jane cares for her children

1 ▪ Jane, Child and Adolescent

Jane Frances Frémyot was born in Dijon, the second daughter of a family designated "nobility of the gown," a status earned from public service. At eighteen months she lost her mother through childbirth. Jane, a more avid learner than her brother, studied reading, writing, and arithmetic with him, and also mastered the female "accomplishments" of dance, music, and sewing. From her father she learned intense ardor for Catholic doctrines.

As a teenager, she lived with her sister Marguerite in a distant part of France to avoid the dangers of religious conflict. There she resisted the unsavory influence of a servant and the marriage overtures of a non-Catholic suitor.

Her father arranged a marriage for her at twenty with Christopher de Rabutin, Baron de Chantal, who belonged to the traditional "nobility of the sword."

2 ▪ Jane, Baroness de Chantal, Wife and Mother

As a bride, Jane took over the management, long-neglected, of the Bourbilly Castle near Dijon. She governed the estate effectively by example with piety and generous attention to the poor.

The lifestyle of the Burgundian nobility varied by season: in autumn and winter they lived a full social life at home; in spring and summer, the men went to war or to court. During Christopher's absences, Jane limited entertaining and devoted herself to prayer.

Six children, two of whom died at birth, were born to the happy and loving couple.

• Bourbilly Castle, two views

• Monthelon castle

• Jane de Chantal as widow, 1608

3 ▪ Jane, Widowed Baroness

In 1601 Jane's husband Christopher was mortally wounded by his cousin in a hunting accident. Jane was plunged into desolation, but rallied to care for her four children. She found it very hard to forgive the unintentional murderer.

Jane placed herself under the direction of a religious who prescribed a rigorous spiritual regime. His mandates, coupled with her own eagerness to give herself completely to God, created in her a tense state of interior captivity. She was further troubled by the urging of her family to re-marry. At the insistence of her father-in-law, accompanied by a threat to disinherit her children, Jane went to reside at his castle, Monthélon, near Dijon. There she endured "a seven and a half-year purgatory." The old Baron had fallen under the influence of a servant-mistress who had borne him five children. Jane and her children were treated with great disrespect which she accepted with equanimity.

In the midst of this humiliation, intensified by the strictures of her director, Jane found solace in her first encounter with Francis de Sales in 1604. Jane had returned to Dijon to hear the famous orator who was preaching there during Lent. There was immediate mutual recognition——each had previously been given a vision of the other——and several meetings followed.

During a pilgrimage made by Francis and Jane to the Shrine of Saint Claude in 1604, he became her spiritual director. Here Jane found affirmation for a previous mystical experience in which she had heard a voice saying, "You will enter the church only through the Gate of Saint Claude." She began a time of deepening simplicity, gentleness, and conformity to the will of God, all undertaken with liberty of spirit.

4 ▪ Jane, Mother Superior

Throughout the difficult years of her widowhood, Jane had longed for the quiet of a convent, where she could enter deeply into the mystical prayer to which she was drawn. Eventually, she attained her desire in the Visitation. However, the demands of forming and nurturing her sisters, of overseeing the administration of the burgeoning order, and of settling her children in life often drew her out of silence and solitude.

She governed as a tender mother, modeling, in the midst of many demands and problems, fidelity to the rule and compassion toward others.

Her intense mystical love inspired Francis, especially as he penned the Treatise. Over the years, the relationship of director/directee evolved into a nourishing reciprocity, with Jane adding distinct shape to the spirituality called Salesian. She infused community life with tenderness; she faced her inner darkness and temptations, which lasted forty-one years, with courage and loyalty to her own experience, keeping her spiritual life deeply hidden. Her prayer became a simple wordless presence before God.

Through the deaths of her children and early companions, she bore herself with gentleness and equanimity. The death of Francis in 1622 left Jane with responsibility for the Order. Her natural talent for organization, combined with deep trust in God, enabled her to guide the Visitation in the establishment of over eighty monasteries.

Her strength lay in her continual fiat to the will of God.

• Jane listening to Francis; first meeting, 1604

• La Bonne Dame, in the parish church at Monthelon

2

BIRTH OF
THE ORDER

SAINT FRANCIS DE SALES

AND

SAINT JANE DE CHANTAL

• Francis de Sales giving the Rule and Constitutions to the first three sisters

1 ▪ Preparation of Jane for Religious Life

From 1604 until 1610 Francis and Jane saw one another only a few times. Their relationship grew largely through exchange of letters. Only the letters of Francis have survived, but his responses give many clues concerning Jane's writing. He counseled the young widow to find peace the midst of dryness, anxiety, and temptations.

2 ▪ Call to a New Religious Institute

In spite of Jane's eagerness to devote herself entirely to God, duty compelled her to care for her four young children and to attend to her elderly father and father-in-law. Francis, even as he counseled her to be patient, used the time in evolving his own plans.

He was conscious that many devout women, desirous of consecration to God, lacked the physical health demanded by the rigors of the strict religious congregations of the era. Widows and those somewhat advanced in age were also excluded from existing monasteries.

He had found in Dijon what the author of the Wisdom Books of the Bible "had not found in Jerusalem"—a valiant woman! Francis would build a new form of dedicated life around Madame de Chantal.

On Pentecost Sunday, 1607, after testing Jane's docility to the call of God, Francis announced his plan to found with her a new institute of religious life.

3 ▪ Family Conference

Jane had made arrangements to have her son educated with his cousins at the home of her father. Her oldest daughter had married Bernard de Sales, Francis's brother, and had planned to go to Thorens to be guided by her mother-in-law. The death of Francis's mother had made it advisable for Jane to go to Annecy to be near the young bride.

Jane intended to bring her other two girls to the convent with her. (Little Charlotte died suddenly before this could occur.)

Thus, it was agreed, when Francis met with Jane's father and brother on October 15, 1609, that the obstacles to Jane's entry into religious life had been removed.

Her father, especially, lamented that she would have to leave Burgundy in France in order to be near the guiding hand of Francis in Savoy, but it was understood that she could return to France when family needs required this.

4 ▪ Farewell Scene

Jane bade a tearful goodbye to her father and brother on March 29, 1610. Her adolescent son, Celse-Bénigne, chose to stage a dramatic scene by blocking the doorway. Jane continued to move forward with tenderness and strength.

Her father blessed her, saying, "Go then, my dear daughter, wherever God calls you, and let us both stem the flow of our justified tears in order to pay greater homage to the divine will."

Jane set off from Dijon with her daughters, Marie-Aimée and Françoise, and with a woman who would join her in the foundation, Jeanne-Charlotte de Bréchard. They arrived at Annecy on April 4.

An unexpected delay in obtaining a dwelling place for the venture resulted in the establishment of the convent on Trinity Sunday, June 6, 1610. This was the Feast of Saint Claude, a consoling fact which connected the foundation with the previous vision of Jane.

• Jane, 1636, Turin portrait

5 ▪ Entrance into La Galerie

That evening, Francis gave Jane and her companions a summary of the Constitutions written in his own hand and blessed the neophytes. They set off toward La Galerie, so named because of a second-story porch or gallery along the side of the house.

Many townsfolk joined them, creating a significant procession through the streets. They were welcomed at the house by Anne-Jacqueline Coste, a simple, devout woman whom Francis had met years before in Geneva. She would become their "Out-Sister." In the chapel, Jane cried out, "This is the place of our delight and rest."

6 ▪ Early Days

The sisters soon donned simple garb, later changed for a more becoming habit. They began study of the Little Office of the Blessed Virgin, which was, even though a simplified version of the Divine Office, formidable enough for women not schooled in Latin.

Prayer formed the center of their lives. These women, once waited on by servants, devoted themselves to domestic tasks. Francis came often to talk with them in a outdoor space called "The Court of the Conferences. "

• *The courtyard of the Conferences at the Galerie House, Annecy*

• *Galerie House chapel*

So delightful was their life that the sisters might have been happy without adding to their number. But others joined them until each of the two bedrooms housed three sisters, and four others slept in the hall. By 1612, they had to leave the outgrown Galerie.

Names were suggested for the new congregation—"Daughters of Saint Martha," "Oblates of the Virgin." By midsummer of 1610, the founders agreed upon "Visitation of Holy Mary," a name not meant solely to refer to visits made by the sisters to the sick poor. Rather, Francis chose Visitation because he "found in this mystery a thousand spiritual insights" which shed light on the spirit he wanted to establish in his institute. The name spoke of worship, adoration, thanksgiving, prayer, relationship, and the hidden mutual service of women.

• *Former monastery where Francis de Sales died in Lyons, Bellecour area*

7 ▪ Profession of Vows

After a year as novices, Jane and her first two companions pronounced simple vows of poverty, chastity, and obedience. Jane spontaneously cried out a verse from the Psalm 132, "This is my resting place for ever and ever," and those assembled in the tiny chapel responded, "Here will I dwell, for I have chosen it."

8 ▪ Foundation at Lyons, 1615

At the request of the Cardinal Archbishop of Lyons, Monsigneur de Marquemont, a foundation of the Visitation began in that city. Francis had created the Visitation as a simple diocesan congregation without the strict cloister and other canonical regulations of existing orders. When the Archbishop insisted on traditional structures, Francis accepted a number of modifications, for he wished the Visitation to grow beyond the little Duchy of Savoy and spread into France and beyond.

In 1618 the Visitation became a formal religious order with papal enclosure and solemn vows. Francis insisted on maintaining a few of the original designs--the Little Office of the Blessed Virgin (rather than the Divine Office, with its Latin often badly mangled) and the name Visitation, which reflects hidden mystery and littleness.

Some persons have felt that the original plan of Francis was totally lost. But he had never envisioned a modern apostolic congregation. From the beginning, visits to the sick poor were limited and meant to be an outward expression of a life of contemplation.

After a short period of adjustment, Jane and the sisters accepted them peacefully as "the will of God's good pleasure."

9 ▪ Expansion of the Visitation

The Order spread quickly across France. After Annecy and Lyons, foundations were made at Moulins, Grenoble, Bourges, Paris, Monferrand, Nevers, Orléans, Valence, Dijon, Belley, and Saint-Etienne en Forez--thirteen monasteries established by 1622, during the lifetime of Francis de Sales.

The spread of Visitation continued rapidly, with over eighty monasteries established before the death of Jane de Chantal. Most of these were in France; one was in Fribourg, Switzerland in 1636, and one in Turin, Italy, in 1638. Fribourg is the only monastery founded during Jane's lifetime which still stands on the original property.

3

SPIRITUALITY

SAINT FRANCIS DE SALES

AND

SAINT JANE DE CHANTAL

• *Ex-voto after the healing of Saint Jane Frances de Chantal*

1 ▪ Rule and Constitutions

With the establishment of the Visitation as an order came the need for a Rule. Francis chose the Rule of Saint Augustine because "his writings are sweetness itself."*

The Constitutions, composed by Francis, designate the purpose of the institute: "This Congregation has been formed in such a manner that no great hardship may deter the feeble and infirm from embracing it, there applying themselves to the perfection of divine love."

The usual monastic practices of sleeping on boards, keeping vigils, perpetual abstinence from meat, and long fasts were not prescribed; in fact, they were prohibited.

Onlookers referred to the Visitation as "The Descent from the Cross." But, in the words of the Founder, "Charity and the force of an interior devotion must make up for all that." The Constitutions call each sister to total self-surrender.

2 ▪ Structure

The Order of the Visitation has a monastic structure, with each autonomous house presided over by a major superior elected by the sisters for a three-year term renewable once. Sisters generally enter religious life, experience formation, spend their lives, and die within the same monastery.

*Quotations are beloved phrases from Francis de Sales.

3 ▪ Evangelical Counsels

Visitation Sisters vow poverty to cut off the "powerful attraction of possessions to dissipate the soul." They vow chastity, "as a wonderful means of belonging completely to God—heart, body, spirit, and emotions." They vow obedience as a means of submitting to God's will through the will of the superior.

4 ▪ Characteristics

Francis urged Visitation Sisters to "ask for nothing and refuse nothing." Thus they are to accept whatever happens to them as the "will of God's good pleasure."

He expressed the special spirit of the Visitation as one "of deep humility before God and of great gentleness towards one's neighbor." The sisters are further called to simplicity, seeking God and God alone, independent of everything else."

A heart pierced with two arrows, surmounted by a cross, and encircled by a crown of thorns was chosen as the coat of arms for the Visitation. This symbol speaks of the centrality of the heart, and thus of love, a focus reaffirmed by the apparitions of the Sacred Heart of Jesus to a Visitandine, Saint Margaret Mary Alacoque in 1671-75. Visitation sisters continue to practice and spread devotion to the Heart of Christ.

They seek union of minds and hearts with one another, in the "bond of love which is the bond of perfection." (Col. 3:14)

They are called to be "Daughters of Prayer," simply attentive to the things of God. Virtues and practices are to be embraced with liberty of spirit, "all through love, and nothing through constraint." The sisters renew this commitment through annual retreats, in common or in solitude.

5 ▪ Apostolic Thrust

As "Daughters of the Church," Visitandines are called to "assist Holy Church and the salvation of their neighbor by prayer and good example." They find their first outreach in the hidden apostolate of prayer.

From the beginning, the Visitation community provided the education for Françoise de Chantal and her companion. Many parents, wishing to have their daughters schooled where they could prepare for First Communion and test their vocations to religious life, brought them to Visitation monasteries for education. The schools grew in number and size until government intervention in Europe closed them.

On the frontiers of the United States, bishops wanted Visitation Sisters to operate schools, and almost all U.S. monasteries began with an educational component. A number of excellent Visitation schools still educate young people.

Communities also serve others by accepting into their cloisters women who wish to spend time in prayer and recollection. Some monasteries sponsor group retreats. Increased social concern is impelling many Visitandines to new and creative ways to reach out to poor and marginalized people.

• Room of Jane Frances de Chantal

4 DAILY LIFE

SAINT FRANCIS DE SALES

AND

SAINT JANE DE CHANTAL

Daily life in every Visitation monastery is decidedly ordinary, with its very repetition helping to provide an environment for recollection in God.

1 ▪ Personal Prayer

Visitation Sisters spend an hour and a half each day in personal prayer. Jane and Francis give counsel for fruitful meditation and for moving into contemplation. In prayer, the sisters are always to follow where the heart leads, whether through dryness or to simple resting in God.

In keeping with the request of the Sacred Heart to Saint Margaret Mary, the sisters honor the First Fridays of each month by keeping a vigil of adoration before the Blessed Sacrament.

• *Annecy community, Exposition of the Blessed Sacrament*

• *St. Louis, USA*

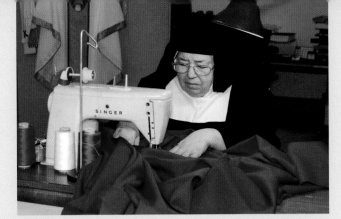

2 ▪ Eucharist

Eucharist is celebrated as the high point of each day in the monastery. The Sisters prepare carefully for "full, active, and conscious" participation in the liturgy. In communion with the entire Body of Christ they pray for the whole world.

3 ▪ Liturgy of the Hours

Translation of the Divine Office into vernacular languages has made this treasure easily available to Visitandines. Through the Psalms the sisters express adoration, thanksgiving, penitence, and supplication for themselves and others. This prayer is simple and open to all.

Morning Prayer and Evening Prayer serve as hinges of the day. Other parts of the Office Readings, Daytime, and Night Prayer—punctuate the remaining hours so that no other activity can become a total preoccupation.

4 ▪ Spiritual Reading

The sisters find nourishment for their interior life in prayerful reading of Scripture as well as spiritual classics and contemporary works. Recent research, translation, and publication have made available much material by and about their Founders. Spiritual reading occupies a half hour each day.

5 ▪ Community Life

Visitation Sisters are called to be a family, helping one another in simplicity and love to discover their gifts and limitations and to serve the common good. The sisters make every effort to be "humble, sweet, cordial, and open," with one another and find asceticism in their striving for genuine love.

6 ▪ Work

Visitation Sisters stand in solidarity with their lay brothers and sisters in bearing the burden of labor, manual or intellectual. They perform, according to their strengths and aptitudes, tasks directed towards the community's needs.

The sisters strive to be diligent and responsible, taking appropriate initiative, and seeking to acquire the knowledge, skills, and professional formation to accomplish their tasks well.

Work provides the sisters with balance in their lives, a share in the work of creation and redemption, an opportunity for collaboration and service, and a wholesome asceticism.

7 ▪ Silence

Silence is observed during most of the day outside of recreations. Necessary business is conducted quietly and tranquilly so that the sisters may retain a spirit of recollection, ever conscious of God's presence within them.

• Tyringham, USA

8 ▪ Meals

Simple meals, often accompanied by spiritual reading, are eaten in common

9 ▪ Leisure and Recreation

Visitation Sisters recreate together every day to provide relaxation and to foster a true family spirit. All participate, sharing their gifts, humor and happiness in one another. They take turns reminding the others of the presence of God in their midst.

Occasionally, there are days of special celebration such as jubilees or other family occasions. These, too, nourish community life and joy in one another.

10 ▪ Announcements

Each day all members of the community assemble for announcements. At this time the superior or any sister may communicate information, prayer intentions, and directives for the smooth operation of the monastery. The sisters use this time to seek permissions from the superior and to arrange matters among themselves.

The superior closes the announcements with words to send forth the sisters with a spirit of renewal and mutual charity for their regular activities undertaken in obedience.

• Rockville, USA

• This cross near the Castle of Sales marks
the place where Francis had a vision
of a future congregation

THIS IS THE PLACE OF OUR DELIGHT and rest. St. Jane de Chantal

• The Windsock Visitation
by Michael O'Neill McGrath

5

THE VISITATION AND ITS MISSION TODAY

1 ▪ Development of the Visitation

What has become of Visitation during the four hundred years since 1610?

Many sisters have lived quiet lives of holiness. Besides the Founders, one sister, Margaret Mary Alacoque of Paray-le-Monial, has been canonized. Seven sisters of the First Monastery of Madrid who died in 1936 in the Spanish Civil War have been beatified as martyrs. Several others have been designated Venerable.

France saw a great flowering of monasteries, many of which were disbanded during the French Revolution. Some were re-established after the Napoleonic era. No other historical event, including World War II, has so affected the Order.

New monasteries have been founded; others have experienced closure for a variety of reasons. At its fourth centenary, Visitation reaches from Canada to Argentina, from the United States to South Korea.

1 ▪ Presence on Five Continents

Since its beginning the Order of the Visitation has spread through much of the world. (Numbers after each country refer to positions on the map.)

ASIA: One community in Lebanon (1); one beginning in South Korea (2).

AFRICA: Three communities in Burundi (3); two in Rwanda (4); two in the Republic of Congo (5).

NORTH AMERICA and **CENTRAL AMERICA:** Two communities in Canada (6); twelve in the United States (7); nine in Mexico (8); one in Guatemala (9); one in the Republic of Panama (10); two in the Dominican Republic (11).

SOUTH AMERICA: Twelve communities in Colombia (12); three in Ecuador (13); one in Peru (14); two in Brazil (15); one in Paraguay (6); one in Uruguay (17); two in Chile (18); two in Argentina (19).

EUROPE: Seven communities in Germany (20); three in Austria (21); one in Croatia (22); one in the Czech Republic (23); four in Poland (24); one in Hungary (25); one in England (26); one in Ireland (27); nineteen in Spain (28); three in Portugal (29); thirty in Italy (30); twenty-one in France (31); one in Belgium (32); two in Switzerland (33).

The mystery of the Visitation, as recorded in the Gospel of Luke, portrays communication and friendship between women. In the absence of juridical bonds, this mystery has inspired union among monasteries and linked them with Annecy, as their "Holy Source."

In 1952, the Holy See joined the monasteries of each area together into federations. While the federations have no authority, they give mutual support and make official the relationships which have always existed in the Order.

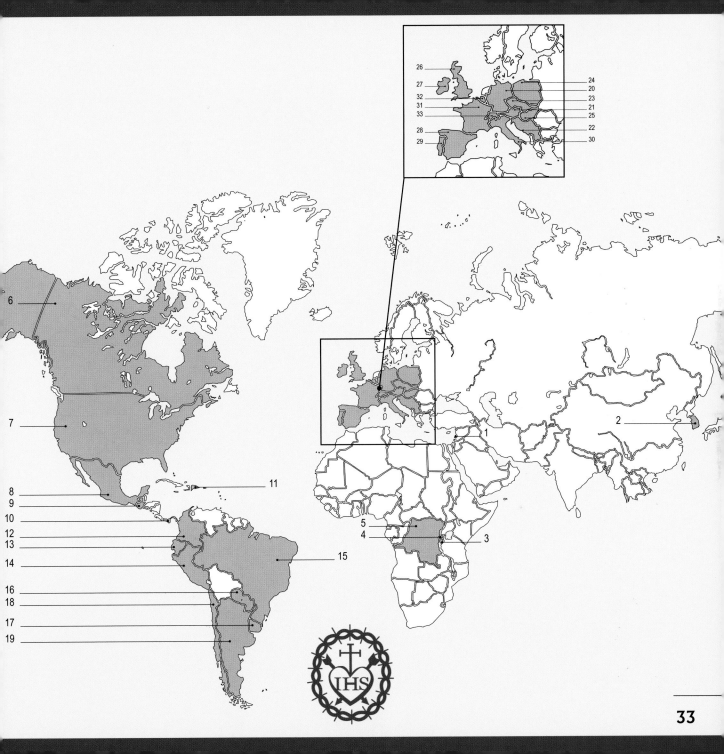

French community

Canadian community

Chilean community

Italian community

Mexican community

Congolese community

American community

*German
community*

Colombian community

*Spanish
community*

Portuguese community

*Swiss
community*

35

3 ▪ The Mission of the Visitation in the Church

Francis de Sales, a strongly pastoral bishop, designated the Visitation Sisters as "Daughters of the Church." Today they understand their primary mission as expressed by the Second Vatican Council: "Through them…the Church truly wishes to give an increasingly clearer revelation of Christ. Through them Christ should be shown contemplating on the mountain… (*Lumen Gentium* 46).

Visitandines also recognize their call to relationships, signaled by the mystery of the Visitation and modeled by Jane de Chantal. The call to justice spoken by Mary in her *Magnificat* and Jane's caring service to others encourage them to seek collaboration. Visitation Sisters, not founded for any particular work, have traditionally reached out in ministry to meet the needs found at their doorsteps.

The 400-year-old marketplace spirituality of Francis and Jane fits well with the present emergence of the laity's role in the Church. There exists today a strong impetus from both religious and laypersons toward varied forms of mutual nourishment within Salesian Spirituality.

• *Statue of St. Francis de Sales*

My soul proclaims the greatness of the Lord,
My spirit rejoices in God my Savior…
He has cast down the mighty from their thrones
and has lifted up the lowly.
He has filled the hungry with good things,
and the rich he has sent away empty.
He has come to the help of his servant Israel
for he has remembered his promise of mercy.

Luke 1:46-54

• Basilica of the Visitation, Annecy

6

THE GREAT SALESIAN FAMILY

SAINT FRANCIS DE SALES

AND

SAINT JANE DE CHANTAL

1 ▪ Continuing Influence

The spirituality lived and promulgated by Francis de Sales and Jane de Chantal extended far beyond the walls of the Visitation monasteries. The literary work of Francis reached countless devotées, especially among the laity.

Personal contact influenced Saints Vincent de Paul and Louise de Marillac and continued to permeate the Vincentians and the Daughters of Charity.

Pierre de Bérulle, Founder of the French School, shared Francis's passion for Church reform, though with different emphases. Later members of the School also reflect Salesian influence in their communities—the Oratorians, the Sulpicians, and the Good Shepherd Sisters.

The centrality of the Heart of Christ in Salesian spirituality culminated during the late seventeenth century in the full-fledged devotion to the Sacred Heart proclaimed by Saint Margaret Mary Alacoque and disseminated by the Jesuits.

2 ▪ Missionaries of Saint Francis

Father Pierre-Marie Mermier, with the support of the Bishop of Annecy, and in covenant with several other priests, began the Missionaries of Saint Francis de Sales in 1838. Their original goal was to re-Catholicize the Chablais region of France. Their headquarters, the castle of Les Allinges, had been Francis's also, during his missionary years there. Their activity has since spread primarily to India. They are best known in the Western world for their many publications of Salesian works.

3 ▪ Salesians of Don Bosco / Sisters of Mary Help of Christians

Francis de Sales, whose native Savoy included the Piedmont area of northern Italy, is still a favorite son of Turin. When John Bosco, a young priest, gathered Turin's street boys around him and attracted priests to the work, he named his Oratory for his patron Francis. The congregation, known as Salesians of Don Bosco, embraced the ideals of love and gentleness.

Maria Mazzarello began a parallel institute for neglected girls. Various groups following the steps of Don Bosco constitute one of the world's largest religious families.

4 ▪ Association of Saint Francis de Sales Salesian Missionaries of Mary Immaculate

In Paris, Father Henri Chaumont guided Madame Caroline Carré de Malmberg with Salesian principles through family difficulties. Laywomen gathered around her as Daughters of Saint Francis de Sales. The group has evolved into two branches, the lay Association of Saint Francis de Sales, and the sisters, Salesian Missionaries of Mary Immaculate.

5 ▪ Oblate Sisters of Saint Francis de Sales
Oblates of Saint Francis de Sales

Guided by Father Louis Brisson and Mother Mary de Sales Chappuis, chaplain and superior of the Visitation in Troyes, Léonie Aviat reached out to working girls in the industrial city. Her followers, the Oblate Sisters of Saint Francis de Sales, embrace the Salesian virtues of gentleness and zeal.

Urged on by Mother Mary de Sales, Father Brisson also began a congregation of men dedicated to the spirituality of Saint Francis de Sales and to its spread. When blocked by the French government, the Oblates of Saint Francis de Sales developed a worldwide outlook in their preaching and teaching, motivated particularly by the "Direction of Intention," the prayer which begins each activity by dedicating it to God.

• Looking toward the Lake of Geneva from Les Allinges

• Francis de Sales, Jane de Chantal, Fr Louis Brisson, Mother Mary de Sales Chappuis, Mother Francis de Sales Aviat

7

THE VISITATION ORDER IN THE UNITED STATES

SAINT FRANCIS DE SALES

AND

SAINT JANE DE CHANTAL

1 ▪ The Foundation of the Visitation Order in the United States of America

In its American beginnings, the Order of the Visitation reflects the dynamics of a new nation, on a new road. The original members experienced many challenges in an era when Catholics were only beginning to breathe freely, negotiating an environment that was sometimes hostile, yet rich in opportunities. Like the leaders of the nation and of the Church at this dawn-time, these women had to make their way independently. As history continued to unroll, and the nation and the Church developed, the Visitation responded to needs in new places.

When a religious order takes root in a new land, it is usually founded by a motherhouse that can sustain it until it is able to function on its own. This was not the case with the Order of the Visitation in America. It took form in the United States during the late 1700s and the early 1800s, when the upheavals of the French Revolution and the ensuing Napoleonic Wars were causing the suppression of religious life. At least 110 European houses of the Order were destroyed or profaned.

Much as a fledgling community in the New World might desire it, no European house could offer aid or direction. Monasteries that might otherwise have fostered the budding American establishments had been confiscated by the government, their communities separated and in disarray.

- Bishop Leonard Neale -

The initial foundation of the Visitation in the United States was the work of Bishop Leonard Neale (1746-1817). He succeeded his cousin, John Carroll, as the second Archbishop of Baltimore, in 1815.

Neale was born at Chandler's Hope in Port Tobacco, Maryland, into the local gentry. He enjoyed almost all the advantages that the Colonies had to offer, with one exception: religious freedom. Maryland had been founded with freedom of worship for all, but in 1655 the political party then in power restricted that freedom. All would

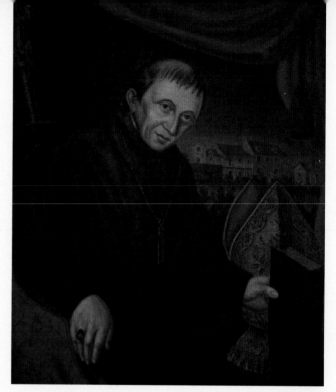

• *Rt. Rev. Leonard Neale, 2nd Archbishop of Baltimore. The Georgetown Visitation monastery is in the background. Painted in 1817 (Neale posed for the picture the night before he died.)*

have freedom of worship except Catholics and Anglicans. Catholic schools were banned, and Catholic places of worship were kept as inconspicuous as possible. With few opportunities for Mass, the Neale family was fortunate in being located only three miles from St. Thomas Manor, where the Jesuits maintained a chapel.

When Mass was unavailable, people turned to "Manuals of Prayer," the popular devotional guides of the era. One popular volume contained lengthy excerpts from The Introduction to the Devout Life. Thus, from his earliest years, Leonard Neale was immersed in the writings of its author, St. Francis de Sales. As an adult, Neale kept both The Introduction and the Spiritual Directory, also by St. Francis de Sales, with him always.

1 All documents quoted in this article are preserved in the Georgetown Visitation Monastery Archives. Each is a file located in RGII and RGIII (Record Groups II and III), History of the Visitation in the U.S. and Foundational Documents.

Because Catholic schools were forbidden, wealthy Marylanders frequently sent their children abroad to be educated. Like many such youngsters, at about ten, Leonard sailed across the Atlantic to St. Omer's, a Jesuit school in French Flanders. As recounted in Georgetown's Convent Book, young Leonard, "having been inclined from early youth to embrace a religious life, and having resolved to dedicate himself . . . to the service of Almighty God in the holy Ministry . . . was ordained a priest in the Society of Jesus.[1]"

Father Neale went to England after Pope Clement XIV suppressed the Society of Jesus in 1733. There he labored as a secular priest before volunteering for mission work in the jungles of British Guiana.

In Guiana, the missionary Neale had a mystical experience. In a vision he saw a long line of women garbed in black moving toward him. He heard a voice—whether in prophecy or command is not recorded—saying, "You will erect a house of this Order." Flanking the procession were two other figures, one male, one female. Father Neale did not recognize either. He had never encountered a picture of St. Francis de Sales or St. Jane de Chantal. Only thirty years later, when someone sent him a holy card picturing both saints, did he recognize these co-founders of the Order of the Visitation as the people in his vision.

At the time, he could not identify the people in his vision, nor the name of the order he was to establish.

- Philadelphia -

Assigned to Philadelphia in 1793, Mr. Neale (as priests were then called in the United States) became acquainted with a young Irish immigrant named Alice Lalor (later known by the religious name Mother Teresa Lalor). He saw in her, and in two other women, never named, the nucleus of a religious community. The three agreed to unite in an establishment dedicated to prayer and the education of young women. The bishop rented a house and, in the words of Georgetown's Convent Book, in 1797 the women

. . . began the laudable work under the conduct of Mr. Neale, who designed that they should open a school for the education of young

ladies, and with confidence he trusted that Almighty God would manifest his Divine Will with regard to this infant establishment, which was commenced solely for His honor and glory.

The community, however, was literally short-lived. That year an epidemic of yellow fever devastated the city, killing 24% of the population. Anyone who could flee left the area, but the three friends stayed to minister to the children. Alice Lalor survived; her two companions succumbed to the disease. She had nursed them day and night with the utmost care, she had prayed with them as they died, and she prepared their bodies for burial.

After that, she remained alone in the house, a dangerous situation in a city where so many were dead or dying, and looting and rioting were rampant. At night she got, as she told later generations of Georgetown sisters, "a woman to keep her company, not because (as she has assured us) that she was afraid, but from prudent precaution." Then she too came down with the fever, and Mr. Neale advised her to return to her family. Abandoning herself to Divine Providence, Alice Lalor returned to her parents' home. She waited and she prayed. Their first attempt to establish a group of religious women had failed.

- Georgetown -

Two years later, Father Neale was appointed president of Georgetown College, on the bank of the Potomac River. Soon after his arrival, he wrote to Alice Lalor, asking whether she were willing to try again. With a companion, the widow Maria Sharpe, and Sharpe's teenaged daughter, she joined Neale in Georgetown. This was a valiant move, because anti-Catholic sentiment was strong in the area, and the inhabitants of Georgetown had reached an equilibrium that they did not want threatened. With some local sentiment against the Poor Clares already in the area, the Catholics of Georgetown feared that the presence of more sisters would upset their non-Catholic neighbors, stirring up trouble. They begged the priest not to introduce another group of religious there.

• First seal of Georgetown Visitation Monastery

• Georgetown physics lab/class circa 1930-1940

Yet Alice Lalor and Maria Sharpe considered that it was God's will that they accept the challenge, and they set out for Georgetown by stagecoach. They took up residence with three Poor Clare nuns, refugees from the French Revolution, who were attempting to establish a school for the girls of the area but without much success. After a few months Maria McDermott, a Philadelphia widow, joined them. Mrs. McDermott had a bit of money, her "dowry," and Father Neale used it to purchase a separate house, next to the Poor Clare convent, for Alice and the two Marias. The price was $1250.

The three women began their own school for poor children, and the neighbors, who were quickly won over by their cheerful demeanor, christened them "The Pious Ladies." They marked June 24, 1799, as their foundation day—the day the school opened.

Six months later, the government of the United States moved to Washington, also on the Potomac. The new community and the capital of the United States of America were born and came of age simultaneously, and in the same city. And, as time went on, the Visitation would begin to influence that government through the wives, daughters, sisters and cousins of Senators and Congressional Representatives—and even of several Presidents—who had been educated at Georgetown Visitation.

In 1800 Father Leonard Neale was consecrated co-adjutor bishop with right of succession to Bishop John Carroll of Baltimore. He maintained his residence at Georgetown.

• Drawing of the first day school, June 24, 1799. Painted from memory by one of the first sisters.

- Becoming Visitation -

As the Pious Ladies began to establish a routine of work and prayer, it became necessary to determine what formal rule they would adopt. Already in Philadelphia, Leonard Neale had discussed Salesian thought with the women. In Georgetown the Visitation rule became a matter of serious study. Books were scarce, but he gave Alice Lalor his copies of the *Introduction* and the *Directory* to read; she shared them with her companions. They read the books under his tutelage, and they prayed over them, finding in them, as recorded in the Annals of Georgetown Visitation, ". . . a nourishment they vainly sought elsewhere." Bishop Neale, for his part, had become more and more convinced that the Salesian spirit of humility, gentleness, and love of one's neighbor was the spirit to which these women were called. According to a manuscript in the Georgetown Visitation Archives:

> It was now his most ardent desire that this new establishment should . . . form a branch of the Order of the Visitation, for although he was ignorant of the rules and customs of that order, the meek and amiable spirit of its saintly founder, whose writings he had often perused, raised it in his estimation and he justly thought that the saint of these latter ages had instilled into the hearts of his daughters that spirit of humility and meekness that had characterized him, that love of God and charity for his neighbors which had marked his whole life. Such

did Bishop Neale wish to be the spirit of that order which he desired to establish. He wished, too, that its members should be particularly consecrated to the Mother of God.

Although the founding members longed for formal affiliation with the Visitation Order, political turmoil in Europe made communication with an established Visitation house impossible. The absence of formal ties did not, however, daunt them. They followed a modified Jesuit rule (having no access to a copy of the Visitation rule) and wore modest secular clothing (not knowing what the habit looked like). Most important, Bishop Neale continued their religious formation in the spirit of St. Francis de Sales.

Once the charism had been identified, once they were certain that God had called them to be Sisters of the Visitation, the Pious Ladies would not be swayed from their purpose: to become true daughters of St. Francis de Sales and to seek full union with the Order of the Visitation.

In the next few years, many people pressured them to join other orders. Some suggested that they affiliate with St. Elizabeth Ann Seton's Daughters of Charity. One wealthy family offered to finance the monastery and supply Ursuline sisters, who had establishments both in New Orleans and in Canada. Meantime, communication with European houses was impossible. The French Visitandines had been forced to disperse, and the Georgetown sisters were horrified to discover that a book sent to them from Louisiana—Part II of the *Lives of the Early Mothers*—had actually belonged to the Third Visitation Monastery of Paris: it had been stolen when mobs looted their convent.

During this period, anti-Catholic feeling was common in the United States, and it would grow stronger, fed by both the sensational literature of the era and the growing nativist sentiment aroused by widespread immigration. *I Leaped Over the Wall*, a lurid tale by a supposedly escaped ex-nun, was a best-seller that fomented this religious prejudice. It would culminate in physical violence, with mobs burning

• *Tomb of Mother Teresa Josephine (Alice) Lalor (right), in Georgetown Visitation's crypt*

convents. When a young student at the Ursuline convent-school in the South died of fever, the sisters there had to allow rioting neighbors to exhume her body, in order to prove that rumors that she had been abducted for immoral purposes were untrue.

Bishop Neale felt that the spirit of St. Francis de Sales, marked by gentleness and humility, was the one best suited to counter the climate of the age. Faced with a hostile environment, the Pious Ladies attempted neither to conquer nor to avoid it. Their Salesian spirituality led them, instead, to accept their circumstances with simplicity and even love. They could not have done more to disarm their critics.

By 1804 the Poor Clares had returned to France, selling their little treasure-trove of books to Bishop Neale to help finance the journey. Tucked back into one of the larger volumes was a tattered copy of the Rule and the Constitutions of the Order of the Visitation. At this great discovery, the Pious Ladies were amazed to find how closely their way of life corresponded to the rule that Francis de Sales had actually written. The differences were mostly in severity; the fledgling American Visitandines were practicing much more physical penance than he had asked of his sisters.

When at last, years later, French and Swiss Visitandines finally arrived to explain the Visitation customs and ceremonies fully, the European sisters were able to embrace their American sisters, recognizing them as true and authentic Sisters of the Visitation. The women from Europe wrote to their home monasteries that they "were charmed with the good order established in this house. The recollection is remarkable and the profound silence which reigns herein reminds us of that which was observed by the ancient fathers of the desert."

Throughout the years, Bishop Neale continued trying to contact English or French Visitandines. Frustrated by these fruitless attempts, he finally, "following the impulse of my mind," and "according to God's will," appealed directly to Pope Pius VII. The bishop sought authority to incorporate the Pious Ladies of Georgetown into the Order of the Visitation.

In 1816 the Pope granted the request. He empowered the second Archbishop of Baltimore to admit the women, who had "with the greatest spiritual fruit, gathered themselves together under the institute of St. Francis de Sales," to the solemn profession of vows. The convent at Georgetown was officially raised to the

• *Georgetown window: St. Jane receives the Rule from St. Francis de Sales*

rank of monastery, and the sisters were acknowledged to be full members of the Order of the Visitation of Holy Mary, with all the rights and privileges that such an affiliation entailed. There were thirty-five members in the community.

In a letter dated March 6, 1817, just two months before his death, Archbishop Neale wrote to the Visitation monastery at Annecy, which he mistakenly believed still existed. (That monastery would not be reorganized until 1822.) In this narrative he explained in detail all the steps he had taken to secure the union of the Georgetown monastery with the Visitation Order during the long years the sisters had waited to be recognized as true Visitandines, and he spoke of the disappointments they had suffered when effort after effort to communicate with the Order had come to nothing. Finally, he expressed the confidence in God's Providence that had sustained them through those trials:

Feeling full of conviction of soul that this house was accepted by Almighty God, and, that it was destined to be regularly united with the other houses of the Visitation, I adored the designs of heaven and was taught to hope against hope. In this humble submission of soul, we persevered.

In their perseverance, in their abandonment to God's will, in their spirit of humility and gentleness, they had not only established a monastery, they had also created a climate in which that monastery, and other religious houses as well, could flourish.

In 1829 another pontiff, Pope Pius VIII, ratified the special foundation at Georgetown, suggesting some changes in structures and discipline that local conditions seemed to demand. The Pope granted the nuns permission to conduct their schools and make certain modifications in cloister to serve the greater good in American society. One adjustment was minimum use of bars and grills lest Protestants form the impression that the nuns were imprisoned. Certain other slight changes were allowed in deference to American customs, e.g., three meals a day instead of two. In his rescript the Pontiff declared that none of these modifications "shall prevent them from being considered Nuns of the same Institute, who follow St. Francis de Sales as their Founder and Leader."

There are striking parallels between St. Francis de Sales's foundation of the first Visitation house at Annecy and Bishop Leonard Neale's foundation of the first house in the United States. Both were rooted in a bishop's attempt to provide for the people of God in his own jurisdiction, within the context of their own particular circumstances and their own needs. Both studied the women who had responded to God's call, taking time to discern what spirituality they were called to. Given Leonard Neale's devotion to the ideals of St. Francis de Sales, and the Georgetown sisters' commitment to embodying them, it is not surprising that the American Visitation authentically reflects the spirit that reigned in the Gallery House at Annecy.

- Visitation in the Nation's Capital -

By now the Georgetown sisters had two schools, an academy for paying students and a much larger "poor school" or "Benevo-lent School" for the poor. As their work became known, visitors began to knock on the monastery doors.

The spirit in which the sisters welcomed their guests did much to educate the public about nuns in general and Visitation sisters in particular. Soon, like their "Holy Mother," St. Jane de Chantal, they began to be called to the parlor, where their cordiality generated much good will. As the Annals tell it, "Protestant ladies ask sometimes to see us in the parlor, and make many inquiries through curiosity, having no idea of our manner of life; they commonly go away well satisfied, and admitting that we are very happy."

Since they were located close to the seat of government, and the women who visited them were often the wives of important officials, the sisters' simple, open hospitality and their obvious joy and intelligence produced wide-ranging effects. A few of the women who came to the parlor later sought instruction. (President Tyler's second wife Julia and her daughter Pearl were baptized in the Visitation Chapel.) Most of the students in the school were not Catholic, and many converted to Catholicism. All visitors learned something about Salesian spirituality, if only by osmosis.

The mere presence of the Pious Ladies in the nation's capital did much to dispel suspicion about Catholics. "The Ministers of the Lord," one sister wrote in the Annals, "doubtless to encourage us in the work, continually assure us that our monastery serves as a buckler to holy Religion against the calumnies hurled by its enemies against Religious, Priests, and Catholics in General."

The Salesian spirit so evident in the sisters' acceptance of their own situation led, ultimately, to public acceptance of them— and to a surge of interest in Catholicism in general. This same effect would be noted in other cities and parts of the country as the Visitation expanded in the United States.

- European Influence -

As unrest in Europe settled down, a few of the many letters Archbishop Neale had sent to the French houses reached their destinations. Much to the Georgetown community's joy, they began to receive replies from their sister houses abroad.

• *Georgetown Visitation 1829*

The First Monastery of Paris had been restored in 1806, fourteen years after its dissolution. In a letter dated May 12, 1816, the French sisters wrote:

> Our surprise has been the greater as we were utterly ignorant of the existence of a monastery of ours in that part of the new world. It would be highly pleasing to us, most dear Sisters, to be made acquainted by yourselves with the origin and progress of your Establishment; not indeed so much for the gratifying of our curiosity, as to nourish that Union and sincere Affection which should reign among all our houses and was so expressly recommended by our Holy Founders.

In November they contacted Georgetown again.

> It is nearly a year that we have been informed by some Jesuit missionaries that there existed a house of our Order at Georgetown in the United States of America, and that the sisters of that house needed the books that belong to our Institute. Though we have no correct knowledge of that Establishment, still to contribute all in our power to the glory of God, and the extension of our Holy Order, we send to your charities whatever we have been able to procure of those Books. . . .

They then describe the destruction of their former convent, including the loss of all their own books, and report that they have had the bookstores of Paris searched to find whatever they could for the American sisters. They also report that "The Bishop of Baltimore had requested the said missioners to have silver crosses made and sent to him of the same form and description as those which we wear, and also to send him a complete habit of the Order." The sisters in Europe responded with whole-hearted generosity: the books and a doll dressed in full habit arrived in Georgetown in November of 1817, and the crosses sometime after.

The year 1829 brought joyous developments. Three European sisters arrived in Georgetown in order to train the American sisters in the customs and ceremonies of the Order. The monasteries of Fribourg, LeMans, and Valence had each sent a sister. Mother Madeleine D'Arreger, of Fribourg, was named superior of the group of travelers. When they arrived in the city, the Georgetown sisters begged Mother Madeleine to assume the office of superior of the house; Sister Agatha Langlois replaced the American novice mistress.

- New Foundations -

Within weeks, Mother Madeleine ordered the construction of a new monastery building; the sisters were badly overcrowded. She then tackled the problem of finances; the monastery had more sisters than it could support. In an effort to solve that problem, and with a sincere desire to spread the Order in the New World, D'Arreger wrote to all the bishops in the country, stating the Visitation's desire to make foundations in their dioceses. Bishop Michael Portier of Mobile, Alabama, was the first to accept the offer. Mother Madeleine herself led a group of Georgetown sisters to answer his call, sailing to Mobile in 1832.

Just a year later, in 1833, Bishop Joseph Rosati of St. Louis invited the Georgetown sisters to make a second foundation—in Kaskaskia, Illinois, at that time a prominent town. That Visitation, relocated to St. Louis in 1844, became the parent of the St. Paul Visitation (now Mendota Heights).

• *Mobile*

• *Mount de Chantal, near Wheeling, west Virginia*

The history of the Visitation in the United States now became *a series* of new foundations. Georgetown established four new schools and monasteries before the Civil War: first in Baltimore in 1837, then in Frederick, Maryland in 1846; in down-town Washington (Washington, D.C.-Bethesda) in 1846; and in Catonsville, Maryland, in 1852. These houses, in turn, made foundations of their own, and the Visitation began to spread across the United States. Today's monasteries in Wheeling and in Brooklyn were founded by sisters from Baltimore: Wheeling in 1848 and Brooklyn in 1855.

• *Brooklyn*

- Keokuk: A European Foundation -

A wave of immigration brought increasing numbers to the eastern part of the country, and people began to move westward. With the population surging toward the Mississippi River and beyond, the demand for Catholic education in those areas became urgent.

• *Monastery of the Visitation - Keokuk, Iowa, in 1853*

Mathias Loras (1792-1858) had come from France to the United States in1828. After ten years serving in Mobile with Bishop Portier, he was named the first Bishop of Dubuque, Iowa. Familiar with the Visitation community that Georgetown had established in Mobile, and with loving memories of the Visitation community near his home in France, he petitioned the French community in Montluel, France, to found a monastery and a school in Keokuk, Iowa. Great was the anticipation among American Visitandines when Montluel agreed!

The Montluel community had originally planned to stay at Georgetown to learn English, but their itinerary changed and they went directly to the St. Louis house. There they attempted both to master the language and to gain some understanding of life and culture on the American frontier. They departed from St. Louis a larger group than they had arrived, with some of the St. Louis

sisters joining them to help them adapt to unfamiliar terrain. The Keokuk foundation opened in 1853.

Like the other original America foundations, the Keokuk monastery found it necessary to branch out. It opened a house in Ottumwa, Iowa, in 1864, and in Maysville, Kentucky, the next year. The sisters who had remained in Keokuk moved to Suspension Bridge, New York, and then on to Wilmington, Delaware (1868). In 1999 that community relocated to Tyringham in the Berkshire Mountains of Massachusetts.

The American population shifted from east to west and from place to place. Some cities seemed destined to be hubs of activity and some to be backwaters. But that could change at a moment's notice: a railroad might be routed through a town, or a town created around a railroad. Gold might be discovered, or oil; the great grain fields of the prairies and the mills necessary to grind their harvest might draw both workers and more affluent owners to a particular area. The Visitation followed where the people who needed them led. Monasteries were established, divided, closed and merged. The flexibility that St. Francis de Sales and St. Jane de Chantal had modeled allowed the Visitation to follow as God's will was made manifest.

• *The graves of first six sisters buried in the catholic cemetery in Keokuk, Iowa. Photo taken in 2002.*

In 1895 Mother Alexandrine de Butler, Superior of Annecy, visited the United States to assist the Wilmington monastery as it closed its school to become a strictly contemplative house. She invited any of the American houses that felt called to do so to give up their schools and become totally enclosed. Several monasteries made that choice: those in Bethesda; in Riverdale, New York; and in Richmond, Virginia (now in Rockville, Virginia). When a group of

Georgetown sisters wished to pursue a completely contemplative life, they opened a house in Toledo, Ohio; Toledo eventually established a foundation near Atlanta, Georgia (now in Snellville).

When the Visitation of Mexico City, founded by Mobile in 1898, was forced out of the country by religious persecution in the 1920s, the sisters transferred to Philadelphia, forming a purely contemplative community there. The other United States houses retained their schools.

- The Federations -

The desire for uniformity among the houses, contrasted with the overwhelming need for the monasteries that did have an active apostolate to honor God's call for them, led to a great deal of anguish. With the publication of the papal decree *Sponsa Christi* in 1951, the Church moved to create federations within a world-wide confederation of Visitation monasteries. The tension between a desire for uniformity on the one hand, yet the call of some monasteries to an active ministry on the other, led to a great deal of anguish. In the United States, two federations were formed.

The First Federation in the United States, those houses which are totally contemplative, include, at this writing, Mobile, Rockville, Philadelphia, Toledo, Snellville, and Tyringham. Georgetown; St. Louis; Mendota Heights, Minnesota (formerly St. Paul); Brooklyn; Wheeling; and Minneapolis form the Second (US) Federation.

Minneapolis is a new expression of the Visitation charism in the United States: it was founded in 1989 by the Second Federation as a whole rather than by an individual house. Located in an inner-city neighborhood, it provides a safe and prayerful presence—especially for women and children—in an impoverished area.

• A group of Visitation Sisters gathered at Georgetown Visitation Preparatory School for a Mass in late June, 1999, celebrating the school's bicentennial. It was the first Catholic school for girls established in the thirteen original states. Over 90 sisters from thirteen convents throughout America and one from England arrived for the event, where they were joined by students, parents and alumnae. Cardinal Hickey celebrated the anniversary Mass, and a symposium followed.

Despite some cultural and geographical diversity, all the houses, in both federations, remain tightly knit. One collaboration came in the aftermath of the Second Vatican Council's call for the use of vernacular languages in the liturgy. The Visitation commissioned Fr. Marcel Rooney, OSB, to compose a version of the Office for American English. Workshops to train the sisters to sing the Liturgy of the Hours brought all the nation's Visitandines together in the late 1970s and early 1980s. Knowing one another, learning to appreciate the histories of all the monasteries, their common goal of Living Jesus, in the spirit of Sts. Francis and Jane—all these bring American Visitandines to realize their unity in God's diverse and beautiful world.

Yearly Salesian conferences, retreats, the fostering of Salesian thought and spirituality among the laity—these are some of the means God offers to help the communities grow in the gentleness, humility, and joy of the Visitation. The Visitation in the United States is indeed of one mind and heart. The Sisters of the Visitation of Holy Mary have both lived and shaped the American experience and the Salesian experience for over 210 years. The labors of the past, kept alive by the spirit of all of our Holy Founders, will carry them into God's future.

May God Be Praised!

2 ▪ The Federations in the United States

A twentieth-century development in the structure of religious life has both challenged and enriched the Visitation in the United States in recent decades. For nearly three and a half centuries, each monastery was founded in total autonomy. Though organizationally separate, the autonomous foundations enjoyed the sense of being a spiritual family. They had "no bond but the bond of love which is the bond of perfection."

In the aftermath of the Second World War, however, Pope Pius XII took steps that were to modify that independent tradition. He was seeking to alleviate the dire poverty afflicting many European contemplative monasteries. To strengthen their support systems, the Vatican's Sacred Congregation for Religious called for the formation of regional and national federations in the decree *Sponsa Christi*, issued on August 15, 1951.

For the Visitation, there was also to be a worldwide confederation, made up of nineteen federations. Vatican authorities appointed the superior of Annecy as the first superior general of the Confederation. This structure contradicted the firm intention of St. Jane de Chantal, who had adamantly opposed any suggestion of having a superior general.

Two forms of cloister, or "papal" enclosure, were established: major and minor. The latter allowed those communities with an apostolate, such as a school, to incorporate it in a portion of the monastery.

Monasteries in the United States were divided according to the form of life observed: the First Federation for the purely contemplative and the Second Federation for those with an active ministry. The superior of the oldest house in each federation was named president of the respective federation.

During the Confederation's short life, the superior general visited all the houses and promoted mutual communication and assistance. The Confederation was abolished by Rome in 1963. However the federations continue to collaborate.

In the United States, sisters of both federations first met in St. Louis in 1968, to discuss Salesian spirituality and to exchange histories. They did so again in Vienna, West Virginia (1971), in Winona, Minnesota (1974), and in Mobile, Alabama (1984).

The federations held five joint workshops at Conception Abbey to enhance the singing of the Divine Office. Other gatherings addressed the revision of the Constitutions. Responsibility for the health care of elderly sisters whose monasteries had closed was accepted by the Second Federation. Stella Maris, a care facility with a monastic setting, was provided in Maryland, close to many eastern houses of both federations.

Each federation has experimented with common novitiates, with mixed results. Cooperation on formation programs, gatherings for newer sisters, and vocation promotion continue. The Internet makes more sharing of intellectual and artistic resources possible.

The Second Federation has met frequently about long-range planning for further collaboration and on a professional basis as educators of young women. These interactions have so bonded the federation that the sisters consider themselves to have one heart and soul. A major theme within the Second Federation is how best to hand on the Salesian charism in Visitation schools. Together the federation has formulated a structure, which can be implemented locally, to continue the charism, especially in schools where no sisters are available for administration.

Programs for associates, neighbors, companions, and other lay collaborators exist in most monasteries under a variety of names, another way of sharing the charism. Annual meetings for sisters of the Second Federation, and sometimes for their lay associates, challenge and stimulate growth in the theology, spirituality and practice of Visitation life.

Each federation holds an assembly every six years to elect a federation president and her council and to discuss individual monasteries' needs. The closing of monasteries is a burden lightened by the support of the federations, which offer assistance in relocating sisters and managing the communities' assets.

Sisters usually participate in the significant events of one another's monasteries. A major event for the Visitation in the United States was the bicentennial of the first American foundation, Georgetown, in 1999. It drew Visitandines of both federations from around the nation and catalyzed much further collaboration. The annual Salesian Conference is open to members of both federations. Working together on plans for the celebration of the Visitation Order's 400th anniversary has enriched communities and the federations.

The vision of Pius XII in 1951 has proved a blessing for the Visitation communities in the United States. Autonomy remains intact, but the spirit of St. Jane and St. Francis is alive and strong as a result of the union of hearts among the sisters of the federations.

• *A group of sisters of the First and Second Federations assemble on the front steps of the chapel for a photograph during the workshop held in Mobile in 1983.*

In 1799, on a hill overlooking the Potomac River, three "Pious Ladies"—Alice Lalor, Maria McDermott and Maria Sharpe—settled in a small house on a plot adjacent to Georgetown College. Father (later Archbishop) Leonard Neale, the college president, was their spiritual father. United in their desire to consecrate their lives to God, they also dedicated themselves to educating young women.

The original members adopted the Jesuit rule. Not until 1816 were they formally professed as Sisters of the Visitation, a privilege that Archbishop Neale obtained for them from Rome.

Alice Lalor and her companions were attracted to the words of St. Francis de Sales. In his Introduction to the Devout Life, they found the spirit they could identify as their own: a spirit of liberty, flexibility, optimism, simplicity and a common-sense approach to life. Salesian spirituality suited a fledgling group of pioneer sisters carving out a new life as religious in a young nation.

Above all, these Americans appreciated the charism of the Visitation, its genuine humility before God and great gentleness in the service of others.

A unique characteristic of the Young Ladies Academy (later named Georgetown Visitation Convent and now Georgetown Visitation Preparatory School) is its permeation by the sisters' life and spirit, flowing into all facets of school life.

||||| GEORGETOWN

If these walls could speak, the aged bricks of Georgetown Visitation would recount an amazing story of courageous women of faith and vision who worked as a community to build an institution that, unique in its origins, still shares its heritage over two hundred years later.

• Crypt beneath the Chapel. Sarcophagus on pillars is Leonard Neale's tomb. Raised sarcophagus on floor is that of Father Cloriviére. Most important: tombstone visible to the left rear is that of Mother Teresa Lalor, foundress of this house.

• Visitation's founders hall after the fire – note charred beams. Looking up from third floor.

The school has fostered a strong tradition of offering one's best efforts to establish a challenging educational program on a solid Christian base and to empower students to meet the demands and challenges of the rapidly changing and morally complex worlds into which they step upon graduation.

The Convent Annals document rapid growth. In 1830 there were 53 sisters and approximately 150 students in the Academy and another 100 in the sisters' "poor school." A new monastery was built in 1832; a new school building was completed in 1873. This building was totally destroyed in 1993 by a fire which left only the four brick walls standing.

The Alumnae Association began in the early 1890's in preparation for Georgetown Visitation's 1899 centennial.

Josephine Cobb's 1894 salutary address demonstrates the contemporary pulse imparted by contemplative women who educated students to realize their "equal abilities, although tradition still denies us the full exercise of them.... We have succeeded as well as the sterner sex in the paths which they thought were theirs alone."

The patterns of life represented at Georgetown Visitation during its first century have continued throughout its second and into its third century. As in its early history, the effects of wars, depressions and periods of prosperity continue to affect the monastery and school.

At one time the school had four elementary grades, a high school and a junior college. The secondary school continues to flourish. The elementary grades ceased in 1948, and the junior college, begun in 1920, closed in 1964. The resident school closed in 1975.

• Chapel of the Sacred Heart, circa 2000. Altar is made from burnt wood salvaged from the fire of 1993

As the school has grown, the religious community has decreased. In 2008 there were 17 sisters and 479 students. The sisters have welcomed the partnership of dedicated lay women and men who have brought a high level of professional competence and a steadfast spirit of loyalty to the spiritual traditions of Georgetown Visitation. Many, through long years of service to the school, continue the sisters' tradition of stability and commitment that distinguish Visitation. Vision and foresight have consistently characterized the monastery and the school.

One dominant thread which has sustained Georgetown Visitation in meeting its challenges is a sense of God's guiding providence. Both the religious community and the school have rested in that providence and trusted its direction for 209 years.

This is the firm base upon which Visitation was founded; it has stood firm through the vicissitudes of time, and it is the base upon which Visitation will operate in the future, continuing to educate young women of faith who will make a difference in the worlds they enter, sharing the gentle strength and vision which they have received.

• Sisters' cemetery in use since 1880. This is one of three burial spots on the monastery grounds.

Soon the sisters moved into a five-room farmhouse. On January 29, 1833, Bishop Portier came to offer Mass for the feast of St. Francis de Sales and to reserve the Blessed Sacrament. This day is considered the date of foundation, though enclosure was established on December 8, 1833, after a monastery had been built.

These Visitandines had come from Georgetown, led by Mother Madeleine Augustine d'Arreger of the monastery in Fribourg, Switzerland. Ill health and Mobile's climate took their toll, so Georgetown sent five replacements in December 1833. They were led by the dauntless Sr. Mary Margaret Marshall. Her appointment as superior broke with custom, as she was a lay sister.

Despite fires, tornadoes, war, epidemics and other disasters, the community grew, liberally assisted by Bishop Portier and the good people of Mobile and New Orleans, as well as by other Visitation monasteries. After the Civil War, the Empress Eugenie of France donated 1000 francs, which was sent to Annecy for the purchase of winter habits and veils. Throughout the nineteenth century, the Mobile sisters had close relationships with monasteries in France, visiting back and forth, borrowing money, turning to France for the repair and purchase of sacred vessels, vestments, and artworks. Six Mobile members transferred to Le Mans in 1867; two sisters from Paris spent two years assisting with the academy.

| | | | | | MOBILE

• De Angelis Cottage, 1st Visitation Monastery in Mobile, 1833

In the waning hours of 1832, four Visitation nuns disembarked at the wharf in Mobile to be met by Bishop Michael Portier. He welcomed them to his young diocese to conduct a school for the daughters of Catholic families in the Gulf Coast areas.

• Sisters' 1st-prize needlework, 1885 World Exposition

• Lourdes grotto, dating to 19th century

The Mobile monastery made a foundation in Mexico in 1898, then welcomed its members—more than forty—fleeing the Mexican Revolution in 1926. Those sisters eventually relocated to Philadelphia.

The monastery prospered into the early twentieth century, but the era of the Second World War brought difficulties which altered the community's circumstances. No doubt the founding members had a vision which sustained them through hardships. Their vision may not have extended to the latter half of the twentieth century, which saw the closing of the school and the undertaking of a new ministry.

More stringent requirements for academic accreditation and a diminishment in vocations led to the closing of the high school in 1948 and of the grade school in 1952. With these closings came the dismantling and disposal of much that had been built up in 120 years: furnishings, equipment, antiques, choir stalls, organ, pews, and even the cows—all were sold or given away.

Property was bought for the sake of privacy; property was sold to finance needed repairs and renovations. The newest building, the pride and joy of all in 1902, had become dilapidated and was demolished. The swimming pool was filled in. Candy-making and altar-bread work became significant sources of income.

• Entrance hall of Visitation Gift Shop

To continue serving the Church, to make good use of the facilities and to be self-supporting, the sisters explored the possibility of opening a retreat facility. Visitandines from several monasteries generously contributed their expertise to help establish this new apostolic work. Inexperienced but undaunted, and trusting entirely in Divine Providence, the community courageously converted the academy into a retreat house and undertook the necessary administration and other tasks. The facility enabled the community to host meetings and workshops for other Visitandines and a banquet for the North American College's 2004 alumni reunion.

In the 1980s, the conversion of the "chaplain's cottage" to the Visitation Shop—featuring gifts, religious articles, and books—provided both a ministry and a significant income source. Friends of the community staff the shop. Major renovations to the living quarters, roof, and chapel met current requirements. Parts of the retreat facility were refurbished.

Notable events have included joyous sesquicentennial celebrations in 1983, the journey to New Orleans with the Atlanta Visitandines for Pope John Paul II's visit, Hurricanes Ivan and Katrina, and the publication of two revised histories of the monastery and academy.

Pondering the future, the sisters often recall St. Jane de Chantal's encouragement: "Have great courage and you will see the glory of God increasing in your house like the glow of a beautiful dawn."

• The stained-glass window under the chapel dome _____

But Bishop Rosati replied that his huge northwestern diocese had room for a Visitation elsewhere. If the sisters would consider going to Kaskaskia, fifty miles from St. Louis on the Illinois side of the Mississippi River, there would be an opportunity. He had just appointed a parish priest there, and the Menard and Morrison families had long desired a school for their daughters. Mother Madeleine Augustine agreed.

Seven sisters and a postulant left Georgetown on April 17, 1833, and began their journey west. They went to Baltimore by stagecoach; then they boarded a horse-drawn train to Frederick, Maryland. For the next five days they swayed along in four-horse stagecoaches through the Alleghenies to Wheeling, West Virginia. There they boarded an Ohio River steamboat. On May 3, the feast of the Finding of the Holy Cross, the captain put the sisters off at St. Mary's Landing on the Missouri side of the Mississippi River.

The gentleman who accompanied them crossed over to Kaskaskia and brought back the disconcerting news that no one had received word of their arrival at that time. Because cholera had broken out in St. Louis, the bishop had not been able to contact the people in Kaskaskia. In spite of their intense disappointment and fear, the sisters took an old boat dignified by the name of "ferry" across brown water that was covered with green caterpillars. They had an immediate taste of "the West" and thus began to pioneer on the American educational frontier.

|||||| ST. LOUIS

Mother Madeleine Augustine d'Arreger, superior of the Georgetown convent in Washington, D.C., dreamed of expanding the work of the Visitation in America. She was also faced with an immediate problem: an overflowing community in Georgetown. In 1832 it was a challenge to support all 50 nuns. Mother Madeleine Augustine wrote to Bishop Joseph Rosati in St. Louis and outlined her dreams. She suggested that a group of her sisters establish a convent and educate young women in St. Louis.

It was good that they could not see into the future. Having labored to see the completion of a brick school in 1838, they named it Menard Academy after their greatest benefactor. Then devastation struck. In the spring of 1844, heavy rains caused the Mississippi and Missouri rivers to overflow. By June 21 the waters filled the basement of the new convent and school. The sisters packed everything they had and moved to the second floor. In God's providence, Bishop Rosati and Chicago's first bishop, William Quarter, arrived—along with Father John Timon, CM. They hailed the steamboat *Indiana* on its way to St. Louis. The captain took on the sisters, students, and pianos, harps, stoves, desks, and benches as cargo.

In St. Louis the sisters continued their trek westward, from Mrs. Ann Biddle's mansion on Broadway to Cass Avenue to Cabanne Avenue. Their most recent move was in 1962 to Ballas Road. There the sisters continue their founding ministry of education by sponsoring a school for approximately 680 students from Montessori pre-school to grade 12. Visitation Academy is known for its excellence in academics, spirituality, service and leadership.

In addition they sponsor a diocesan outreach center, the St. Jane Center, begun in thanksgiving for 150 years in St. Louis. The sisters also promote Salesian spirituality, offering a variety of opportunities for faculty, parents, alumnae and friends to live a devout life. And each sister embraces the archdiocese and the world in her individual prayers and in daily communal, liturgical prayer.

• *Students of the class of 1899 with two sisters*

• *Tradition describes St. Jane praying before this statue from Le Mans, France.*

• *Academy window (installed 2000)*

Inspired by the spirit of St. Francis de Sales and St. Jane de Chantal, Bishop Whelan's intention was to establish in Wheeling a school where young women of all faiths would be welcomed. This Salesian attitude of openness to all of God's children has been a guiding principle at the Mount during the 160 years since its founding. Girls from many states and territories came to board at the school called "Wheeling Female Academy." Originally located in downtown Wheeling, in 1865 the school moved about three miles to its present location and was renamed Mount de Chantal Visitation Academy.

The Civil War left many Southern families unable to pay the costs at the academy. With ecclesiastical permission, the sisters began the Mount's first campaign for funds, traveling to Philadelphia and New York to solicit contributions. One person they contacted in New York was Tammany Hall politician Boss Tweed. Touched by the sisters' dedication, he loaned them a carriage and driver and gave them letters of introduction to prospective donors.

The sisters collected sufficient funds to pay construction debts and to establish a "Southern Fund" for financial assistance for pupils from the South. Letters of gratitude from Jefferson Davis and Robert E. Lee are precious artifacts in the Mount de Chantal archives.

In 1867, a small band of Mount sisters under the leadership of Sister Borgia Tubman founded a Visitation community and academy in Abingdon, Virginia. After a move to Wytheville, Virginia in 1902, a declining number of sisters led eventually to the closing of the academy and monastery in 1944.

| | | | | MOUNT DE CHANTAL

• *Chapel dome by Rambusch*

• *The Visitation: 19th-century painting*

Called to the hill country like Mary, eight Visitation Sisters from Baltimore responded to the needs of God's people in western Virginia in 1848. Invited by Most Rev. Richard Vincent Whelan, these courageous pioneers—gracious, compassionate, gentle women—proclaimed the Gospel message by their lives of prayer and presence and their work of education.

• *Students and sisters at recreation (1875)*

Change at Mount de Chantal over the years reflects the changes experienced by American society. In this combined resident- and day-school, students and alumnae from all over the United States and beyond have given the faculty and students a more personal awareness of broad global concerns. The Mount roster has included girls from Latin America, Europe, Africa, Australia, and Asia. In addition to the program for girls in grades five through twelve, since 1970 the Mount has offered a Montessori pre-school for boys and girls, and since 1984 a coed elementary school.

Recent decades have brought hard times to this once thriving Ohio River city. Wheeling has experienced a serious decrease in population and work opportunities, reflected in Mount de Chantal's decrease in enrollment since the late 1980s. In addition, there are physical plant difficulties: heating the 19th- and early 20th-century academy structures requires astronomical dollars; many needed maintenance tasks have been postponed.

In 2008, in a spirit of faith, trust in God's Providence, and openness to his Will in all things, the eight Visitation Sisters who comprise the Mount de Chantal community announced that Mount de Chantal Visitation Academy would close on graduation day, May 31, the Feast of the Visitation.

The press release about the closing that was issued January 18, 2008, stated that Mount de Chantal's 160 years of Salesian education have provided a "legacy of love" and a "celebration of women." This legacy will live on not only in the memories of its alumnae and friends, but concretely in the lives of loving service of thousands of its alumnae. Through these wonderful women and those whose lives they have influenced, the Visitation spirit has spread throughout society in general and in the "little churches" of family and friends.

The eight Visitation Sisters residing at the Mount will continue their primary service of prayer and presence as members of the Diocese of Wheeling-Charleston, which was founded two years after the establishment of Mount de Chantal in 1848.

• *Sister and pupils on porch (1892)*

• *Music Hall windows by Mayer, Munich*

Several days later an unexpected visitor arrived, Bishop John Loughlin of Brooklyn, accompanied by Baltimore's Archbishop Francis Patrick Kenrick. Bishop Loughlin had already brought several religious communities to Brooklyn. He wanted Visitation Sisters to educate young women in their faith and in arts and science, as the Visitandines in Georgetown and Baltimore were successfully doing.

The sisters answered this call, and the first monastery was established on Lawrence Street in Brooklyn with the foundation date of September 24, 1855.

The community moved to two other locations before settling on its current site in Bay Ridge in 1903. This unpopulated section of Brooklyn had an excellent landscape, gardens, and fine trees, enhanced by a magnificent view of the Narrows, Upper New York Bay, Staten Island and the New Jersey coast. The urban environment has since grown to surround the walled enclosure of seven bucolic acres. The monastery remains a peaceful oasis.

Assisted by generous benefactors, the sisters had the beautiful Sacred Heart Chapel constructed, a sacred place of worship for them, their students and Catholic neighbors.

The Brooklyn community has sought to maintain a sensible balance of cloistered contemplative life and the spiritual and academic nurturing of their students. For over a century, Visitation Academy's administration and educational program were in the capable hands of sisters. After the Second Vatican Council, and in light of the increasing demands of education, a re-structuring resulted in the hiring of lay faculty. The first lay principal joined the school in 1996, and the first alumna lay principal in 2002.

|||||| BROOKLYN

• *Sr. Marie de Chantal* • *Sr. Susan Marie*

"FOR THE GLORY OF GOD"

The call for a foundation of the Visitation in the Diocese of Brooklyn came in summer 1855 during a novena undertaken for the pure glory of God. It was the recreation hour in Baltimore's Monastery of the Visitation. During a discussion of novenas, one sister remarked that she had never heard of a novena being made for the pure glory of God. The sisters decided to begin one immediately.

The Salesian charism permeates the Academy, encouraged by a dedicated lay faculty and administration imbued with this spirit and supported by the prayer life of the sisters and their presence in some religion classes.

Visitation Academy's alumnae include many professional women. Of those who entered religious life, the martyred Maryknoll missionary Ita Ford is the most prominent.

The monastery hosted the initial Federation meeting in 1956 and was the first American house visited by Mother Bernard Marie D'Uriarte as Mother General. The first opportunity to make solemn vows made 1963 a spiritually significant year for the sisters.

The community gave hospitality to Eastern European refugees and to bishops traveling to and from the Second Vatican Council.

The monastic annals record the friendship of the Very Reverend J. Francis Tucker, OSFS, over several decades. The visit of Blessed Theresa of Calcutta in 1986 remains a vivid memory.

In 1995 the monastery began a new trend in Brooklyn by displaying a life-sized Nativity scene on the front lawn during Christmastime. Many parishes have since followed suit. The annual Sacred Heart Novena, welcoming the public, remains a central jewel of the community's spiritual life.

The attacks of September 11, 2001, on the Twin Towers in New York deeply affected the Brooklyn sisters' monastic life. They witnessed the event, as the Towers were very visible from the monastery's upper floors. Two graduates of Visitation Academy lost their lives in the collapse of the Towers. That tragic day became the instrument of an intensified prayer life for the sisters.

In 2005, the community celebrated its sesquicentennial. The joyful liturgy on September 24 culminated a series of liturgical celebrations throughout the year for friends and benefactors, alumnae, priests, family, and Visitandines from around the nation.

The Brooklyn community has received new members since the Church's Jubilee Year 2000 and has celebrated four solemn professions since the sesquicentennial. Despite realistic challenges of aging, signs of a hopeful future have emerged.

Visitation Monastery in Brooklyn remains a paragon of simplicity; a hidden haven of quiet prayer and peace within the sophistication of New York City, with sisters dedicated to living the Heart of Jesus in fidelity to the essence of the Visitandine vocation and perseverance in their mission to their students.

• *Sr. Gail*

• *Sr. Mary-Cecilia*

The home purchased for them was situated on the highest hill in Richmond, located in the Church Hill area. It afforded a sweeping view of the devastated city below. How Church Hill got its name is unknown, but it was certainly appropriate for the sisters.

To live inside the walls of Monte Maria is to become deeply aware of the pioneering sisters of the community who, despite enormous obstacles and actual destitution, gave generously of themselves in order that an enduring, living temple of prayer should find its place in the Diocese of Richmond. When the monastery eventually moved from Church Hill to its present location in Rockville, the remains of those Sister Pioneers and those who followed them were also moved. To this day they are honored in Monte Maria's beautiful cemetery, where they are prayed for with loving gratitude.

Bishop McGill desired that, in the heart of Virginia, cloistered religious would pray in a special way for his priests. At his request the sisters also conducted a small boarding school for girls.

To lead a purely contemplative life had always been the sisters' one desire. Not until 1927 did that dream become a reality. A legacy from the estate of Major James Dooley, brother of Sr. Mary Magdalen Dooley, enabled the sisters to close the academy.

For a time they were engaged in the ministry of printing, supplying churches and other institutions. However, it became necessary to discontinue this work because meeting deadlines intruded upon scheduled times of prayer. From then on the community's income has been supplemented by the baking of altar breads.

• Baking altar breads

||||| ROCKVILLE

• Inner courtyard

Monte Maria in Rockville, Virginia, was founded in the Diocese of Richmond in 1866, at the conclusion of the Civil War. At the request of Bishop John McGill, seven sisters were sent from the Visitation Monastery of Baltimore to make a foundation. These founding sisters were Mother Mary Juliana Matthews, Superior; Srs. Mary Louis Williamson, Mary Innocent McAtee, Mary Justina Prevost, Mary Francis de Sales Gahagan, Margaret Mary Kennedy and Mary Pelagia Redding.

At the time of the community's centennial celebration at its original location on Church Hill, no one, including the Sisters, even considered the possibility of relocation. In subsequent years, however, a move became necessary. Obsolete facilities, deteriorating buildings, and increasing dangers in the neighborhood prompted the monastery's friends and advisors to encourage relocation.

A beautiful piece of property for sale in Rockville, Virginia, was brought to the sisters' attention by members of the Cosby family, devoted friends of many years. Secluded, scenic, with rolling hills, green fields, woods, and a peaceful lake, it seemed a setting created for a monastery by a provident Father. The sisters moved into their new home on April 4, 1987, a day long to be remembered.

Members have come to rural Virginia from many states, countries, and cultures, allowing the community to experience unity in diversity. The focal point of Monte Maria is the chapel. Its layout facilitates the participation of the laity in the liturgical celebrations, creating a visible bond of unity with God's people. High ceilings, a massive crucifix, stained-glass windows, and a pipe organ invite all who enter to lift their hearts to God and join the sisters in singing Our Lady's joyous song of praise, "My soul proclaims the greatness of the Lord and my spirit rejoices in God my Savior."

In Rockville, as in Richmond, the monastery continues to be known as "Monte Maria" –The Mount of Mary.

It is the sisters' hope and prayer that those who read this brief sketch of their beloved Monastery will join in begging Our Lady to make her secret visitation to many young hearts, gifting them with a vocation that will enable this monastery to continue its mission of prayer and praise.

• *Chapel – focal point of the monastery.*

• *Our Lady of Fatima shrine*

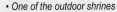
• *One of the outdoor shrines*

Finally, the decision was made. Srs. Marie Mechtilde Pernaud, superior; Marie Anastasia Martin, assistant; and Marie Agnes Journet; and a postulant, Marguerite Bouvard, were chosen. A three-month journey brought them to Iowa on August 11, 1853. Along the way they had spent six weeks in St. Louis. There two Visitandines, Srs. Mary Angela Smith and Mary Beatrice Tyler, joined them to facilitate communication in English.

The community struggled with poverty and cultural differences. The sisters established a school, at times giving their own food to the children. Eight young sisters died of tuberculosis. Several other foundations were made. By 1866 the community had seventeen members.

In hope of thriving elsewhere, in 1866 the community chose Suspension Bridge, New York, invited by Mother Mary Josephine's brother, Father Robert E. V. Rice, the Vincentian superior of the College of Our Lady of the Angels. They had a very slow beginning. Meanwhile, the Diocese of Wilmington, Delaware, had been formed from Philadelphia and was desperate for sisters.

Mother Mary Clementine, the superior, proceeded cautiously, considering the uncertainty of another move. However, Wilmington's newly consecrated Bishop Thomas A. Becker promised spiritual and financial support. The community relocated to Wilmington, where property was made available. Bishop Becker faithfully helped with their spiritual and temporal needs.

On December 8, 1868, the sisters settled into rent-free buildings at St. Mary College. Two years later, they moved to the "Brownstone," better suited to a cloistered community and a boarding school. The school and community flourished.

• Community prays grace before meals in the refectory

‖‖‖‖ TYRINGHAM

• Baking bread for benefactors

• Sr. Anne-Marguerite teaches novitiate class

The Tyringham Visitation has roots in the monastery of Montluel, France. In 1852, Montluel's Mother Marie Therese Pitrat received a letter from Father Jean-Baptiste Villars, requesting a Visitation in Keokuk, Iowa. She hesitated; her community had been re-established for only thirty-three years since the French Revolution.

Problems inevitably arose, however, and prompted Sr. Mary Baptista Mack, who was responsible for managing material needs, to plead with God in prayer. Turning to Scripture, she received this word: "The silver is mine, and the gold is mine, saith the Lord of Hosts. Great shall be the glory of this last house more than of the first, saith the Lord of Hosts; and in this place I will give peace, saith the Lord of Hosts" (Haggai 2:9-10).

God provided, and the success of the school and other apostolic endeavors necessitated an expansion by 1891. Mother Mary Baptista consulted Bishop Alfred Curtis, who had a different suggestion.

Bishop Curtis was counseling a young novice of the Georgetown Visitation, Sr. Mary Joseph Abell, who felt called to religious life but not to teaching. She was willing to endow a monastery that wanted to give up its school and become purely contemplative. Bishop Curtis discussed this idea with Mother Mary Baptista, prudently revealing no details. Assured that the entire Wilmington community would desire it, he facilitated Sr. Mary Joseph's transfer there. Mother Mary Baptista requested a superior from Annecy, and Mother Alexandrine de Butler was sent, along with Sr. Marie Adrienne Frechon.

The Ursuline Sisters assumed responsibility for the school, which today is the successful Ursuline Academy in Wilmington.

Mother Alexandrine trained the Wilmington community in the customs and manner of Annecy. Sr. Mary Joseph's profession ceremony took place on November 21, 1892. She transferred the rights and privileges of foundress to her sister, Miss Frances (Fannie) Agnes Abell. By August 3, 1893, a new monastery was completed.

After a century of growth, the monastery began to show its age. Lovely homes, two schools and a city park surrounded it. Contemplative quiet had become a rarity, and the beautiful gardens on two and a half acres were only a small patch of peace. On November 21, 1989, the sisters voted to search for another site. Initially they wished to stay in the diocese; however, the search carried them through seven states and twenty-three properties to Tyringham, Massachusetts.

While a monastery was being built (1993-1995), the sisters lived in St. Joseph Convent in Pittsfield; the infirmary sisters stayed with the Sisters of Notre Dame de Namur in Worcester. Finally, on December 19, 1995, all reunited in the new monastery.

Today the community is blessed with 133 acres of woods and meadows filled with God's beauty and can truly sing, "God be praised!"

• *Tyringham community, 2008*

• *Sisters' choir*

As usual in establishing a new monastery, experienced maturity balanced youthful energy. Mother Agatha Russell, a strong Irish woman and former superior, exemplified the former; Sr. Clementine Shepherd, newly professed at twenty-two, the latter. Sr. Martina Corbley was the first and only domestic sister in the Saint Paul community. (Archbishop John Ireland would soon outlaw this traditional rank as un-American.)

The sisters traveled by steamship up the Mississippi River for eight days, settling on August 12 in a frame house near the present Lafayette Bridge. Their first breakfast in Saint Paul was delivered by nine-year-old Mollie McQuillan, who immediately became a Visitation pupil and much later, Mrs. Edward Fitzgerald, mother of novelist F. Scott Fitzgerald.

The Visitation Sisters were dedicated to "living Jesus," a spirituality centered on love as taught by Saint Francis de Sales and modeled by Saint Jane de Chantal–one flowing from interiority and characterized by humility and gentleness.

School opened in September. That year twenty-nine girls, aged six to seventeen, enrolled. Extreme poverty required the sisters to move the same chairs back and forth for eating, worshiping, and recreating. In 1876, the superior thought that "the sisters would probably return to Saint Louis." But they did not return.

||||| MENDOTA HEIGHTS

• May Procession

Six Sisters of the Visitation came in 1873 to the fast-growing river town of Saint Paul, capital of Minnesota. Seventeen citizens had pledged financial contributions to bring Visitandines to educate their daughters. Bishop Thomas L. Grace had made the official request to the Visitation community in Saint Louis.

By 1881, the sisters and students had outgrown the original dwelling and had moved one-half mile to University and Robert Streets. In 1889, an impressive castle-like structure opened to house the school, while the sisters lived in a frame house on the property. When an anticipated major donor for the new building died intestate, the sisters were left with a huge debt. The situation was exacerbated when, as a result of the Panic of 1893, many parents withdrew their children from the school.

Somehow, the sisters weathered the financial crisis. Other challenges remained: continual tension between the call of contemplative prayer and the demands of a modern school, need to observe cloister regulations yet educate the sisters, decline of the city neighborhood. This last problem was solved by alumna Clara Hill (daughter of railroad tycoon James J. Hill), who purchased property and erected a new monastery and school on Fairmount Avenue in 1913. There classes became more formal.

Two world wars affected women's expectations and aspirations. Gradually, Visitation's curriculum moved from emphasis on the social niceties of "carriage society" to the academic demands of college preparation. The boarding school yielded to an enlarged day school. Sisters emerged from the cloister to attend graduate schools.

Many young women, wishing to serve God and drawn by the gentle spirit of the sisters, entered the community. The student body also grew. After fifty years on Fairmount Avenue, monastery and school were overcrowded. Property was purchased in Mendota Heights to allow for expansion. After a capital campaign, planning meetings, "garage sales," packing (thousands of library books!) and nostalgic farewells, the sisters moved in 1966 to eighty acres in the country. In the larger facilities, the school program expanded and included the enrollment of young boys.

Even more significant were the changes in religious life called for by Pope Pius XII and the Second Vatican Council. The vernacular in worship led to recitation of the Divine Office (rather than the simpler Office of the Blessed Virgin); cloister was interpreted more broadly; sisters took more personal responsibility for their prayer life; initiative was encouraged; ecological and social justice concerns grew.

New opportunities for women to serve God and the Church eventually led, as in most religious congregations, to departures of sisters and a scarcity of new vocations. With the resultant aging and downsizing have come two positive steps: closer affiliation and long-range planning with other Visitation monasteries through the Second Federation of the United States; and a conscious effort to transmit the Salesian heritage, particularly to the school's lay administration and faculty.

The Sisters of the Visitation in Mendota Heights continue to "live Jesus," serving God and the Church with interiority, humility, and gentleness.

They came at the invitation of Bishop Joseph Schrembs, Toledo's first bishop. Arriving in Toledo on June 30, 1915, the sisters moved into the bishop's former residence on Collingwood Avenue. The next day the Liturgy of the Hours (Office) was chanted. On July 2, the Feast of the Visitation and the First Friday of the month, Bishop Schrembs made the formal establishment of the Visitation in Toledo. He told the sisters they were to "remain upon the mountain top in prayer and sacrifice to plead for the welfare and salvation of souls, particularly for those of his diocese, clergy, religious and laity." Thus was his dream realized to have sisters in his diocese for the sole purpose of aiding the Church by prayer and sacrifice to procure blessings for the priests and the laity.

On Ash Wednesday, February 14, 1918, the sisters moved into their new monastery on Parkside Boulevard (then City Avenue). On June 13 of the same year, the church and altar were solemnly consecrated. In his sermon the bishop told the congregation, "Here will be manifested the glory of the Sacred Heart by the miracles of grace and benediction, obtained through prayer; these are the secrets of hearts here below, and joy of angels above." Three days later he established strict ecclesiastical enclosure.

Eventually, the community began making and distributing altar breads as a source of income. The sisters no longer bake altar breads, but they continue to distribute them to parishes inside and outside the diocese.

||||| TOLEDO

• *Mother Mary Agnes before her entrance at Georgetown*

• *First residence of the sisters on Collingwood Boulevard*

The founding sisters of Toledo's Visitation prepared themselves for the purely contemplative life of this new foundation, and for their special mission in the diocese. Four professed sisters and a novice came to Toledo, Ohio, from the Georgetown monastery in Washington, D.C., in 1915. Because the Georgetown monastery had an academy, the sisters spent a month at the Wilmington (now Tyringham) monastery, which was solely contemplative, to make the transition.

For the mother-foundress, Mother Mary Agnes Faulhaber, the rhythm of Visitation life centered around the Sacred Heart, the Eucharist, and a hidden life of love of God and charity toward the neighbor. She confided to her daughters that, during Holy Thursday night, Christ had told her that this foundation would be "for the manifestation of the glory of his Sacred Heart...."

In promoting this love of the Sacred Heart, Mother Mary Agnes was instrumental in the establishment of the Guard of Honor, the first meeting being held in October 1918. The first public novena in honor of the Sacred Heart took place in 1928. The novena has become an annual event to give glory, love and reparation to the Sacred Heart.

Thirty-nine years to the day that the founding sisters had taken the train from Wilmington to Toledo, history repeated itself. In 1954, Toledo became a mother, sending ten sisters to Georgia to start a foundation of the purely contemplative life. Today that community resides in Snellville, Georgia.

The spirit of self-sacrifice and peaceful surrender to the will of God, so characteristic of Mother Mary Agnes, permeates the lives of her daughters and lives on as a testimony to her humility, life of prayer, and deep union with the Beloved. The glory of the Sacred Heart continues to be manifested throughout the diocese in proportion to the sisters' loving fidelity to the little virtues so dear to their holy founders, St. Francis de Sales and St. Jane de Chantal, and Mother Foundress Mother Mary Agnes.

In 2010, Toledo's Visitation shares with the local diocese in celebrating the diocesan centennial, and with the entire Visitation family in celebrating the 400th anniversary of the original foundation.

In 1898, a Father Rubi, CM, prevailed upon the Mobile Visitation to undertake a foundation in Mexico. Sr. Mary Stanislaus Campbell, former superior of Mobile, was appointed superior of the new foundation. A Señor Escudero offered to finance the venture. On his extensive property the sisters established a small monastery. By December 8, 1898, they had prepared a miniature chapel for the official commencement of the foundation.

However, it was soon necessary to move to Tepexpam, where, in 1905, the community opened a small school. That year Mother Mary Philomena Connelly was elected superior, replacing Mother Mary Stanislaus in accord with the Rule's requirements for limited terms of office. About 1907, Sr. Stanislaus's health started to fail; after a stroke, she asked to return to Mobile, where she died in May 1911. That same month, Mother Margaret Mary Semple was elected.

In 1912, the Mexican Revolution broke out following the fall of President Diaz. Amid the disruptions, the community had to move several times from one location to another in Mexico City.

A Cuban-born former pupil at Mobile, Mother Louise Frances Mitjans, was elected in 1917. Under her leadership, the community was able to settle in an ideal location in Coyoacan in 1918. Here both a monastery and a school were built. The sisters resided there for seven years, the longest time they were able to live in any one location in Mexico.

• *Pope John Paul II with the novitiate sisters of Philadelphia, 1979*

 # PHILADELPHIA

• *Library*

• *Outside chapel*

The history of the Philadelphia Visitation spans two nations and over a century of hardships. The long road to Philadelphia began in Mobile, Alabama.

However, the government of Calles decreed that religious should be expelled from their institutions. Accordingly, in 1926 the sisters had to leave their monastery, don secular clothes, and eventually leave Mexico. They proceeded to Mobile, where they arrived on March 10, 1926.

Now they searched for a diocese that could accept them all. Finally Cardinal Dennis Dougherty of Philadelphia gave the hoped-for permission. However, despite his good will, the Cardinal could offer the community only three row houses on Camac Street. The sisters set about cleaning these slum houses and tried to earn their living by painting, embroidering altar linens, and making vestments. Conditions were so difficult and unhealthy that by 1940, when Cardinal Dougherty notified the community of a property next to his own that was for sale, sixteen sisters had already died of tuberculosis.

With difficulty the community purchased the property. Here the community took on new life. Divine Providence manifested itself early through benefactors and through the Guadalupe Guild, founded by Mrs. Edward B. Dougherty in 1955 and still very active today under the direction of Isabelle Momonee.

Mother Louise Frances Mitjans saw to the erection of a permanent chapel, attached to the main building, in 1959. In 1961, Sr. Clare Marie Rose, former superior of the Brooklyn monastery, was elected superior. Mother Clare Marie was responsible for many improvements, including the building of an infirmary wing in 1965. Other monasteries, notably Toledo, Riverdale, Richmond, and Ottawa also lent sisters at this time. A broken hip, suffered in 1970, gradually limited Sr. Clare Marie's activities. To create a transition, the Archdiocese appointed Mother Mary Gabrielle Muth of Wilmington, the Federation President, as superior of Philadelphia. She served from September 1976 until March 1977. In 1977, with Riverdale's permission, Cardinal John Krol appointed Sr. Frances de Sales Paganelli superior.

What may have been the most memorable event in the community's history occurred in 1979, when Cardinal Krol invited the sisters to meet His Holiness Pope John Paul II on the Cardinal's grounds next door.

A bell tower in memory of Monette Robinson's mother, Blanche LaForest, was erected in 1985.

Since 1984 several superiors have been elected: Sr. Guadalupe Teresa Rizo, 1984-1990; Sr. Frances de Sales, 1990-1999; Sr. Antoinette Marie Walker, 1999-2002; and Sr. Frances de Sales, 2002-2008.

The community hosted the First Federation Assembly that was called in 2005 to elect a successor to Mother Margaret Mary McGuire, Federation President, who had died.

It was now a totally American community, which strove to embody the Visitation charism in the strictly cloistered Visitandine life as required ordinarily by the Constitutions and by Cardinal Dougherty when he admitted the community into his archdiocese.

• *Stained-glass rose window of the Sacred Heart by Gabriel Loire*

• *Sister at prayer in the nuns' chapel (choir)*

||||| SNELLVILLE

The foundress was Mother Francis de Sales Cassidy, a native of Macon, Georgia. She had entered the Visitation of Georgetown in Washington, D.C., in 1912. But she had always prayed that one day she would return to found a Visitation monastery in Georgia. Her prayer and her dream found fulfillment in 1954.

In the intervening years, she had accompanied Mother Mary Agnes Faulhaber to found a monastery in Toledo, Ohio, in 1915. Perhaps this experience was a providential preparation. When Sr. Francis de Sales was elected superior in Toledo in 1954, she was in a position to make the first steps toward a Georgia foundation. Those steps were completed on August 15, 1954.

Bishop Francis Hyland, auxiliary bishop of what was then the Diocese of Savannah-Atlanta, advised Mother Francis de Sales to take her group of sisters to Atlanta, rather than to her hometown of Macon. As her only desire was to have the Visitation Order in Georgia, she gladly complied.

The founding group of ten Visitandines and their benefactors purchased a mansion which had originally belonged to Asa Warren Candler, nephew of the Coca Cola king. The house lent itself quite easily to remodeling. When ready for occupancy, it was blessed, and enclosure was established.

In 1974, the community moved to Snellville, a suburb of Atlanta. It is about twenty-five miles away from the city but still in what is now the Diocese of Atlanta.

• The Chapel

• Outdoor Way of the Cross

The Monastery of the Visitation in Snellville, Georgia, is called Maryfield, a name most appropriate for the year of its foundation, 1954, which was an extraordinary Marian Holy Year.

The community treasures memories of meeting two saints important to the worldwide church. In 1987, they traveled with the Visitandines of Mobile to the Cathedral of St. Louis in New Orleans, for the visit of Pope John Paul II to that city. Remembering a beloved Visitation community in Poland, the Pope recognized and greeted the Visitandines individually, touching each in blessing. He responded particularly warmly to Sr. Mary Josepha Kowalewski, who greeted him in Polish.

Two sisters had the opportunity to meet Mother Theresa, foundress of the Missionaries of Charity, when she visited the convent of her community in Atlanta.

The current monastery is of contemporary architecture. It contains individual bedrooms for each sister, and all else necessary for the Visitation contemplative life.

At the same time, the sisters recognize that the call to holiness extends to each and all.

• *Mosaic created by the entire community*

• *Chanting the Liturgy of the Hours*

• Mater Admirabilis

• Two houses - One monastery

LIVE JESUS
Beholding the cross that embraces

The foundation was unique in being made not by one monastery but by the Federation. Mother Philomena Tisinger, then the Federation president, called it "Our widow's mite . . . . Not one community has any Sisters to spare. We are giving all we have to live on."

The Visitation of St. Louis released Srs. Mary Margaret McKenzie, Karen Mohan, and Mary Virginia Schmidt; the Mendota Heights Visitation released Sr. Mary Frances Reis. Mother Philomena appointed Sr. Mary Margaret superior. The community emphasized that this urban monastery be a place of prayer, fostering reflection with those who work with the poor, gathering rich and poor together in faith, hope and love, and listening to the Lord through the poor and their needs;

- a lived experience of "reverse mission," i.e., receiving from as well as giving to the people, thus revitalizing the charism;
- an island of gentleness amid violence;
- an enrichment for the whole Federation;
- a sign for the poor that they are "worth it."

On October 2, 1989, after ten years of prayerful discernment about responding to the Church's call for a "preferential option for the poor," the Second Federation of the Visitation in the United States founded a new monastery among economically challenged and marginalized persons in Minneapolis. This community was to live interiority and simplicity in an urban neighborhood, in the spirit of Mary's "Magnificat," proclaiming praise and justice.

From a rehabilitated three-story family residence, the founding sisters gradually expanded to a second residence. Their contemplative life centers on the Eucharist; prayer; the Liturgy of the Hours; and welcoming street people, neighbors, and friends. Their ministry includes programs for children, teens and families. They work to build peace, collaborating with lay Visitation associates and faith-filled neighbors in this mission:

...to 'Live Jesus' by being part of this multi-cultural community—to share prayer, hope and God's blessings. Our friends are drawn into a circle of faith that brings us all to a clearer vision of the face of God.

The area's reputation for violence worried others, but confirmations from their "Visitation Saints" released the sisters from fear.

The first came from St. Francis de Sales. The founding sisters had asked God for a dream, in the Biblical spirit, to help clarify the difficult decision on a location. None of them had a dream. When they reported to Sr. Peronne Marie, superior of the Mendota Visitation, about their choice, she said excitedly, "After you tell me your decision, I want to tell you about the most phenomenal dream I had last night." She had dreamt, "It will be north Minneapolis." Then they recalled the words of St. Francis de Sales: "I will visit the hearts of all the Sisters... by visiting the heart of the Superior" (Année Sainte, January 29).

The second confirmation came from St. Jane de Chantal. The realtor had arranged to close the purchase on August 17, the day before St. Jane's feast. The sisters returned from the signing to Mendota Visitation for First Vespers of the feast and found the saint's wisdom in this liturgical text:

Have great courage and you will see the glory of God

increasing in your house like the glow of a beautiful dawn.

The third sign was from St. Margaret Mary. Two days after her feast, and before the sisters had occupied the new monastery, a carpenter discovered a holy card, dated 1942, under a bookcase there. The image of the Sacred Heart and Jesus' "12 Promises" to St. Margaret Mary confirmed their seventeenth-century visionary sister's presence in this new expression of the Visitation, upheld by Jesus' outpoured love.

Other affirmations include new members and many laypersons committed to Salesian spirituality and neighborhood ministry. The sisters live on alms. Many Visitation communities, especially Mendota Heights, generously support a shared response to the "preferential option for the poor."

The Windsock Visitation, painted for the sisters by Br. Mickey McGrath, OSFS, recalls their identity as prophetic followers of God. Radically open to the Holy Spirit, Mary and Elizabeth needed one another's support and companionship. Each responded humbly, gently and in liberty of spirit to God's designs in her life. Such is the way of life to which the Visitation Sisters of Minneapolis aspire.

• *Joy is knowing who you are and whose you are.*

VISITATION MONASTERIES

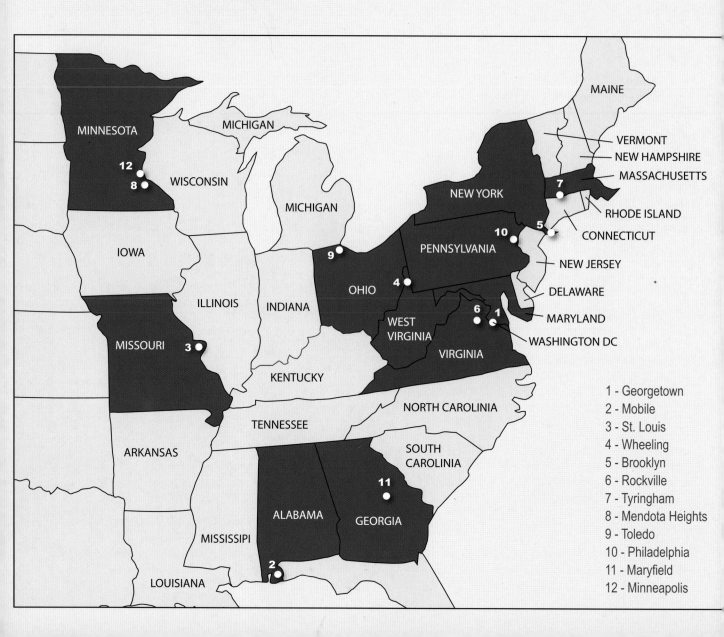

1 - Georgetown
2 - Mobile
3 - St. Louis
4 - Wheeling
5 - Brooklyn
6 - Rockville
7 - Tyringham
8 - Mendota Heights
9 - Toledo
10 - Philadelphia
11 - Maryfield
12 - Minneapolis